Fathers and Sons

Brian Friel

after the novel by
Ivan Turgenev

SAMUEL FRENCH, INC.
45 WEST 25TH STREET   NEW YORK 10010
7623 SUNSET BOULEVARD   HOLLYWOOD 90046
LONDON   *TORONTO*

rian Friel

RVED

Printed in U.S.A.
ISBN 0 573 69107 X

BILLING AND CREDIT REQUIREMENTS

All producers of FATHERS AND SONS *must* give credit to the Author in all programs and in all instances in which the title of the Play appears for purposes of advertising, publicizing or otherwise exploiting the Play and/or production. The author's name *must* appear on a separate line in which no other name appears, immediately following the title of the play, and *must* appear in size of type not less than fifty percent the size of title type.

IN ADDITION: the following credit *must* appear on the title page in all programs and all advertisements of 1/8th of a page or larger:

American Premier Presented at
The Long Wharf Theater

M. Edgar Rosenblum   Arvin Brown
Executive Director   Artistic Director

11 March, 1988

All such billing for Long Wharf Theatre shall be easily readable and not less than 12 points of type.

for Tom and Julie

CHARACTERS

ARKADY NIKOLAYEVICH KIRSANOV — Student (twenty-two)

YEVGENY VASSILYICH BAZAROV — Student (twenty-two)

NIKOLAI PETROVICH KIRSANOV — (Arkady's father; estate owner (forty-four)

PAVEL PETROVICH KIRSANOV — Arkady's uncle; retired guardsman (forty-five)

VASSILY IVANYICH BAZAROV — Bazarov's father; retired army doctor (sixties)

ARINA VLASSYEVNA BAZAROV — Bazarov's mother (fifties)

FENICHKA FEDOSYA NIKOLAYEVNA — Nikolai's mistress (twenty-three)

ANNA SERGEYEVNA ODINTSOV — Estate owner; widow (twenty-nine)

KATYA SERGEYEVNA — Anna's sister (eighteen)

PRINCESS OLGA — Anna's aunt (seventies)

DUNYASHA — Servant in Kirsanov home (twenties)

PROKOFYICH — Servant in Kirsanov home (sixties)

PIOTR — Servant in Kirsanov home (nineteen)

TIMOFEICH — Servant in Bazarov home (sixties)

FEDKA — Servant in Bazarov home (sixteen)

MUSIC

ACT ONE

Scene 1 — Beethoven's *Romance* (for violin and orchestra) in F-major, Op. 50.
Scene 2 — Piano duets. In marching, military style.

ACT TWO

Scene 1 — Beethoven's *Romance* in G-major, Op. 40.
Scene 2 — As in Act One Scene 1.
Scene 3 — *Te Deum Laudamus.*
Scene 4 — 'Drink to me only' (vocal and piano).
— 'Drink to me only' (played on piano-accordion).

Fathers and Sons opened at the Lyttelton Theatre, South Bank, London, on 8 July 1987. The cast was as follows:

ARKADY NIKOLAYEVICH KIRSANOV	Ralph Fiennes
YEVGENY VASSILYCH BAZAROV	Robert Glenister
NIKOLAI PETROVICH KIRSANOV	Alex McCowen
PAVEL PETROVICH KIRSANOV	Richard Pasco
VASSILY IVANYICH BAZAROV	Robin Bailey
ARINA VLASSYEVNA BAZAROV	Barbara Jefford
FENICHKA FEDOSYA NIKOLAYEVNA	Lesley Sharp
ANNA SERGEYEVNA ODINTSOV	Meg Davies
KATYA SERGEYEVNA	Robin McCaffrey
PRINCESS OLGA	Joyce Grant
DUNYASHA	Hazel Ellerby
PROKOFYICH	Antony Brown
PIOTR	Jay Villiers
TIMOFEICH	Peter Halliday
FEDKA	Jim Millea

Directed by	Michael Rudman
Designed by	Carl Toms
Music	Matthew Scott

Presents

THE AMERICAN PREMIERE!

FATHERS and SONS

A New Play by

BRIAN FRIEL

After The Novel by Ivan Turgenev

Directed by
AUSTIN PENDLETON

Set Design by
JOHN CONKLIN

Costume Design by
DAVID MURIN

Lighting Design by
PAT COLLINS

Production Stage Managers
ANNE KEEFE
ROBIN KEVRICK

March 11 - April 24, 1988

ARVIN BROWN - Artistic Director
M. EDGAR ROSENBLUM - Executive Director

THE CAST *(in order of appearance)*

Fenichka	EVE GORDON
Nikolai Kirsanov	RALPH WILLIAMS
Dunyasha	DENISE BESSETTE
Pavel	GEORGE MORFOGEN
Prokofyich	CLEMENT FOWLER
Arkady Kirsanov	MICHEL R. GILL
Yevgeny Bazarov	JAMES ANDREASSI
Piotr	DREW McVEIY
Anna	CARIS CORFMAN
Princess Olga	MARGARET BARKER
Katya	SHELLEY LOVE LATHAM
Vassily	WILLIAM SWETLAND
Arina	JOYCE EBERT
Timofeich	MAURICE BRENNER
Fedka	GARY GREENBURG

ACT I Scene 1: Early Afternoon in May, 1859. The Kirsanov home.
Scene 2: June. The Kirsanov home.
Scene 3: End of June. The Bazarov home.

ACT II Scene 1: Late morning in August. The Kirsanov home.
Scene 2: The following morning. The Kirsanov home.
Scene 3: Afternoon in early September. The Bazarov home.
Scene 4: Early October. The Kirsanov home.

THERE WILL BE ONE INTERMISSION

Casting by Deborah Brown
Wigs by Paul Huntley Productions

*World premiere of FATHERS AND SONS presented at the National
Theatre of Great Britain at the Lyttleton Theatre London, July 9, 1987.*

9

FATHERS AND SONS—Running Props

ONSTAGE PRESET

Inside Permanent Wagon: On ACT I Spikes
1 Piano
  on:
  Lots of music
  Practical Lamp (Plugged)
1 Piano Chair
1 Cello Chair
  near: Cello
       Cello Bow (ditto) on arm ch
1 Armchair
  on: 1 cushion
1 Side Table
1 Long Bench
  on: Cushion
1 Small Wicker Table

On Stage Right Wagon #1
1 Wicker Planter w/Plants

On Off Stage Right Wagon
1 Bookcase

On Stage Left Wagon
1 Wicker Table w/Plants

On Off Stage Left Wagon
1 black chair

ON DECK   *On Act I Notes*
1 Oval Table
  on: Bazarov Cloth (green)
     Kirsanov Cloth (white)

4 Chairs w/covers
1 Armchair U.L.
1 Footstool U.L.
1 Bench S.L.

IN GAZEBO
Rugs and Pillows
1 Knitting Bag S.R.
Knitting (in progress, ready to knit) S L.
Outside:
1 Baby basket on stand
  in: Baby, dressed (head is U.S.)
     Baby blanket
  over: netting
Plants

CHECK: Curtains and window positions

UP RIGHT PRESET (ACT I)
I-1
1 Basket w/laundry — Dunyasha
1 Tray — Fenichka
  on:
  1 Sherry decanter (⅔ full 'black sherry')
4 glasses
1 Tray — Dunyasha
  on: 4 cups
     4 saucers
4 spoons
     1 cup cocoa (full) w/saucer and spoon
     1 creamer w/milk
     1 sugar bowl w/lump sugar
     Sugar tongs
1 Samovar Table — Prokofyich

1 Samovar (½ full hot water)   on wagon
  on: small tea pot w/strong tea
1 Small White lace tablecloth — Dunyasha

I-2
2 Dishes ice cream w/spoons — Arkady, Bazarov
1 Dish ice cream w/chocolate sauce and
  cherry — Arkady
1 Dish ice cream w/spoon — Arkady
1 Tray — Dunyasha oval

UPRIGHT PRESET — ACT II
II-1
3 Rolled maps — Nikolai
4 For change

II-2
1 Tray — Dunyasha large rectangle w/handles
1 Package sandwiches — Fenichka
1 Bottle milk — Dunyasha

II-4
2 Tablecloths (1 arrives after II-2;) sm. on top) —
  Prokofyich — On Piotr tray
3 Side chairs

1 Tray — Piotr — round
  on: 7 Dessert plates
     Dessert spoons
1 wine rack w/3 full bottles 'wine' — Prokofyich
1 Tray — Prokofyich
  on: 7 wine glasses
2 Vases flowers — Piotr
7 Folded napkins — Piotr
1 Watering Can — Fenichka

1 Tray — Dunyasha
   on: 6 Champagne glasses
Champagne coolers Bottle
1 Tray — Dunyasha-little
   on: 3 dishes ice cream
1 Tray — Piotr — big
   on: 3 dishes ice cream
1 Taper to light lanterns

UP LEFT PRESET — ACT I
I-1
1 Book — Pavel-green
2 Empty demis on tray

I-2
1 Book — Pavel
1 Lamp
Ben:
   Ank. tea,
   Bowl & napkins
   Bag 2 tea,
   Bowl & Nap.
   1 Plate cookies
(Fedka's Boots)

UP LEFT PRESET — ACT II
II-1

II-2
1 Green book — Pavel U.C.L. table
1 Roll bandage
1 Medical tool set
1 Bottle medicine
(Pavel's sling, Act I jacket)

Dressing room

II-3 Act II U.L. shop—set in DLV Act I
3 tea glasses (2 w/tea)
3 spoons
3 napkins
1 Jam holder w/jam and spoon
1 tea pot w/hot water
1 creamer and sugarer
1 plate cookies
Tray (big enough to hold above)—Timofeich

II-4
2 new books—Katya U.C.L. table
1 ring box w/ring (may be personal)

DOWN RIGHT PRESET—ACT I AND II
I-1
2 Leather suitcases—Prokofyich
1 Black Suitcase—Prokofyich
1 Small Canvas case—Prokofyich
  in: 1 small book
Scraps of paper, small pencil (cover)
Tray with tea
Silver Tray:
  Big Berry
  2 Sm Berry w/spoon
  Bowl of cookies
  2 Tea
  2 Napkin
Wooden Tray:
  2 Sm Berry w/spoon
  2 Tea
  Teapot
  Jam

2 teas
2 napkins
Plate of cookies

II-1
1 Bunch roses — Fenichka

II-4
1 Table — Piotr and Prokfyich
1 Flask with water
1 Bottle w/gulp

FOR CHANGES:
Maps 1 – 4
Acct. Book
Inkstand
Tablecloths

PERSONALS:
Mr. Andreassi: Roll of Bandage, tools & med.
              Scraps of paper
              Pencil stub
Miss Barker: 1 walking stick
Mr. Morfogen: 1 small bottle cologne (Eau Sauvage)
              ring box w/ring (5)
              Books I-1
                     I-2
                     II-1
Mr. Swetland: Notebook
Mr. McVety: Rag

AFTER I-1

STRIKE:
Samovar
Samovar table

All dishes and trays (only cream and sugar repeat
  cups and saucers, spoons dead)
Cello and bow
Tablecloth from railing
Costumes
Note: Baby basket is dead
        Leather suitcases are dead
        Cello and bow are dead
        Samovar and table are dead
        Laundry basket

SET:
Cello chair to behind piano
2 Espresso cups (w/coffee) saucers and spoons to piano
2 Espresso cups (w/coffee) saucers and spoons to oval
  table
Chair #2 away from table
Chair # 3 away from table and straight on

AFTER I-2

STRIKE:
Onstage armchair
Stool
Covers from table and chairs

SET:
Table to new spikes
I-3 up left props to table

INTERMISSION

U.C. Platform:
  Cello struck
  Demitasse cups on tray struck
  Cookie plate struck
  Piano on new spikes
  Small table on spike

D.S.
  Oval table on Bazarov spikes (U.S.)
  Green tablecloth unstuck with white Kirsonov
  tablecloth on top with:
    Account book
    Inkstand
    Maps 1–4
  Reset chair with chair covers
  Nikolai's hat on #1 chair
  Check skirts
  Armchair and stool on spike

GAZEBO:
  Check pillows and rugs
  Make sure bottle is behind pillow

OFFSTAGE:
  Table is set in D.R. Vom
  Escape steps set with curtains paged
  Doctors bag on bookcase
  Chandelier is up
  S.R. masking flat

AFTER II-1

STRIKE:
Anna hat

SET:
4 coffee cups, saucers, spoons (set #2) to oval table on
    big tray
Cream and sugar (repeat)

AFTER II-2

STRIKE:

Kirsanov cloth (goes to U.R. for next scene)
Chair covers
Armchair (cushions are dead)
Stool

Set:
Table to new spikes
Chair #3 opened up
Chair #2 S.L.
II-3 props (exc. tray) to table
Check doctor bag top book case

THEN:
Set lanterns to off right wagon

AFTER II-3

STRIKE:
II-3 PROPS

SET:
Arm chair
Stool
Cushions to position in gazebo
Check cello chair behind piano

THEN:
Go U.R. to help
Light lanterns

BEN

Unstore Table D.R.

Enter D.R.
   Set armchair, stool, chair covers, maps, table cloth,
     account book, inkstand
   Wine bottle to armchair spikes.
   Set props on bench
   Unstick tablecloth
   Add Kirsanov tablecloth
   Cover chairs and set to spikes
   Set table props
   Set Nikolai's hat (Jim will bring out)
   Cue units to move
   Wash dishes and reset

JIM
Strike chandelier
Strike Arkady's jacket, take to dressing room, pick up
   Nikolai's hat
Bring hat onstage and set on bench
Go to U.S. unit
Move piano to second spikes

Check: Small table back
        Cello, demitasse and tray struck
Watch units reset
Set doctor's bag to S.R. Bazarov unit

DAWN
Set escape stairs
Page curtains

BEN
Unstore table D.R.
Enter D.R.
   Set armchair, stool, chair covers, maps, table cloth,
      account book, inkstand
   Wine bottle to armchair spikes
   Set props on bench
   Unstick tablecloth
   Add Kirsanov tablecloth
   Cover chairs and set to spikes
   Set table props
   Set Nikolai's hat (Jim will bring out)
   Cue units to move
   Wash dishes and reset

JIM
Strike chandelier
Strike Arkady's jacket, take to dressing room, pick up
   Nikolai's hat
Bring hat onstage and set on bench
Go to U.S. unit
Move piano to second spikes
Check: Small table back
        Cello, demitasse and tray struck

Watch units reset
Set doctor's bag to s.r. Bazarov unit

Dawn
Set escape stairs
Page curtains

Fathers and Sons

ACT ONE

Scene One

Before the scene begins bring up the sound of Beethoven's Romance *in F-major, Op. 50, played by NIKOLAI on the cello. Early afternoon in May, 1859.*

The garden-lawn in front of the Kirsanov home. We can see into the living-room U.S. *A veranda runs across the front of the house with two steps leading down to the garden. Some potted plants in front of the veranda. Downstage left there is a gazebo/summerhouse. Various summer seats and stools. (Left and right from the point of view of the audience.) Characters Enter from the left — i.e. the yard, outhouses, servants' quarters off — or from the house.*

NIKOLAI *is playing the cello in the living-room.* FENICHKA *is sitting in the gazebo, knitting a garment for her baby who is sleeping in a pram at her side. She is an attractive young woman with innate dignity and confidence; but because she is no longer a servant and not yet mistress in the house she is not fully at ease in her environment. Occasionally she glances into the pram. She leaves aside her knitting, closes her eyes and sits listening to the music.*

DUNYASHA *Enters left carrying a laundry-basket full of clothes. She is a plump, open-natured, openhearted, practical-minded girl who loves to laugh.*

DUNYASHA. Oh my God, this heat has me destroyed. How do you stick it?

FENICHKA. You should have something on your head.

DUNYASHA. I met the new estate-manager over there at the clothes-line. Do you know him?

FENICHKA. Only to see.

DUNYASHA. He is just so beautiful — isn't he? I could spend my days just gazing at him, with that glossy black moustache and those sleepy brown eyes. Did you notice that beautiful black 'tash?

FENICHKA. Dunyasha! (*DUNYASHA flops down beside her. FENICHKA begins knitting again.*)

DUNYASHA. Honestly. All he'd have to do is raise his little finger and I'd kiss his feet. Anyhow he looked at me and he said, 'Are you going to faint, little one?' All the same that was nice, wasn't it? — 'little one.' And I said, 'What d'you mean — am I going to faint?' 'Oh,' he said, 'your face is all bloated and red.'

FENICHKA. (*laughing*) He did not. That's another of your stories.

DUNYASHA. Cross my heart. (*into pram*) Hello, Mitya. How are you today, my little darling? Are you well? (*She spreads out under the sun.*) Beautiful. This must be the hottest May ever. (*eyes closed*) Is that the big fiddle he's playing?

FENICHKA. You know very well it's called a cello.

DUNYASHA. Sort of nice, isn't it? Bit lonely — like himself.

FENICHKA. Is he lonely?

DUNYASHA. You should know. Not much good for dancing.

FENICHKA. I heard you were dancing last night.

DUNYASHA. Five this morning. Oh, that heat's lovely.

FENICHKA. Any good?

DUNYASHA. You mean did I click? (*She sits up.*) Tell me this, Fenichka: remember all those young fellows

used to be at the dances when you and I went together—
all that laughing and all that fun—remember?

FENICHKA. Yes.

DUNYASHA. Well, where in God's name have they
gone to, those boys? Or haven't they young brothers? All
you see now are half-drunk louts that say things like,
'My God, girl, but you're a powerful armful of meat.'
(*FENICHKA laughs*) It's true. That's what a big clod-
hopper said to me last night. And if it's not the clodhop
pers it's the usual old lechers with their eyes half-closed
and their hands groping your bum. (*She sees PAVEL
entering* L. *with a book under his arm. She gets quickly to
her feet. PAVEL is the typical 'Europeanized' Russian of
the nineteenth century—wears English clothes, speaks
French. His manner is jaded but his emotions function
fully and astutely.*) Jesus, here comes the Tailor's
Dummy! He must have spotted you.

FENICHKA. Don't go, Dunyasha. Stay with me.

DUNYASHA. You're well fit to handle that old goat.
And Dunyasha's place is in the kitchen.

FENICHKA. Please.

DUNYASHA. You're too gentle. Tell him straight out
to bugger off. (*She rises, makes a curtsy to PAVEL and
Exits quickly* L., *leaving her basket behind her. The rela-
tionship between PAVEL and FENICHKA is uneasy. He
looks into the pram and then at FENICHKA.*)

PAVEL. Am I intruding?

FENICHKA. No. Not at all.

PAVEL. Will you be sending into town for groceries
today?

FENICHKA. Yes.

PAVEL. Would you order something for me?

FENICHKA. What do you want?

PAVEL. Tea. Green tea. If you would.

FENICHKA. Of course.

PAVEL. Half a pound would suffice.

FENICHKA. I'll see to that.

PAVEL. *Merci bien.* (*into pram*) Hello-hello-hello-hello. He has very strong fingers. Maybe he'll be a cellist like his father. How do you like your new bedroom, Fenichka?

FENICHKA. I love it. It gets the sun in the early morning.

PAVEL. I see your light on very often in the middle of the night. (*She rises and gathers her things.*)

FENICHKA. That's his lordship—cutting a new tooth. Aren't you cutting a new tooth, you rascal, and keeping your mother awake at night?

PAVEL. Tu es très belle.

FENICHKA. Sorry?

PAVEL. Look—he won't let me go.

FENICHKA. Let your uncle go, Mitya.

PAVEL. Fenichka—

FENICHKA. I think I'll take him inside. This sun's a bit hot for him.

PAVEL. All I want to say is—

(*He gets no further because PROKOFYICH Enters L. He is an elderly retainer, excessively dignified and formal in manner; but now he is so excited, indeed so confused, that he almost runs across the stage and proclaims too loudly to nobody in particular:*)

PROKOFYICH. The carriage has arrived! He's back! Master Arkady is back!

PAVEL. That's early. They must have made good time.

PROKOFYICH. The carriage is here! He has arrived! He has arrived!

PAVEL. A bit of life about the place.

FENICHKA. Yes.

PAVEL. Fenichka, forgive me if—

PROKOFYICH. Master Arkady is back! The carriage is here! Arkady's home from Petersburg! (*PROKOFYICH is now on the veranda and calling into the living-room. NIKOLAI emerges with the cello-bow in his hand. He walks with a slight limp. He is a kind, decent, generous-spirited man, vague and bumbling at times but always fully alert to what is happening around him.*) The carriage is here! Arkady's home! He's back! He's back!

PAVEL. All right, Prokofyich, we hear you.

NIKOLAI. Did you hear the news?

PAVEL. I think so, Nikolai.

NIKOLAI. Arkady has arrived from Petersburg. Wonderful! Where's Piotr? Piotr! Somebody help him with the luggage. Go and meet him, Pavel. (*to FENICHKA:*) He'll probably want something to eat, won't he? Everything's in such confusion. This is no welcome. Piotr! I'm really going to have to reprimand that young scamp.

(*General confusion and excitement. PROKOFYICH rushes off L. DUNYASHA rushes on and picks up her basket.*)

DUNYASHA. (*privately to FENICHKA:*) He has a friend with him! Get out your smelling-salts! O sweet Saviour!

FENICHKA. Take the pram inside, Dunyasha, will you?

DUNYASHA. Wait till you see *him!* A dark god! Jesus, could this be my lucky day?!

PAVEL. Who is he bringing with him, Nikolai?

NIKOLAI. Dunyasha, tell Piotr I want him—

immediately! (*She dashes off with the pram and basket.*) Yes, he's bringing a friend with him — a young man called — called — I'm sorry, I've forgotten, Pavel. I'm really going to sack that boy. (*ARKADY Enters.*) Ah! There he is! Arkady! Arkady!

ARKADY. Father! How are you! (*Father and son embrace with great warmth. Already ARKADY is beginning to resemble his father. PROKOFYICH, cases in his hands, stands in the background and beams.*)

NIKOLAI. Welcome home! Welcome home, graduate!

ARKADY. Thank you.

NIKOLAI. Let me look at you, You're different. Have you lost weight? You're altogether different. Have you eaten? You're pale — that's it — you're very pale —

ARKADY. All that study and all those exams. What I need is a long rest. Uncle Pavel!

PAVEL. Welcome back, Arkady.

ARKADY. It's great to see you. (*They embrace warmly.*) And . . . Fenichka. It *is* Fenichka, isn't it?

FENICHKA. It is.

NIKOLAI. Of course it is.

ARKADY. Indeed. Good to see you, Fenichka.

FENICHKA. And you, Arkady. (*They shake hands and she leaves.*)

NIKOLAI. Prokofyich usually drives so slowly, we didn't expect you until much later. Had you a good journey?

ARKADY. It was all right. I've brought a friend with me, Father.

NIKOLAI. You mentioned that in your last letter. Great.

ARKADY. His name is Bazarov.

NIKOLAI. Wonderful. We'll have a full house again. And wait till you see your bedroom — we've had it all repapered. Pavel chose the colour scheme.

PAVEL. That was a major row.

NIKOLAI. No, it wasn't — was it?

PAVEL. A minor row.

ARKADY. His name is Bazarov — Yevgeny Vassilyich Bazarov. I would like you to make him very welcome.

NIKOLAI. Naturally we'll make him very welcome. Won't we, Pavel?

ARKADY. Our friendship is very important to me.

PAVEL. Did he graduate, too?

ARKADY. Next year. He's doing natural science and medicine. He's probably the most brilliant man I've ever met.

NIKOLAI. Well, the brilliant Bazarov is every bit as welcome as you are . . . well, almost.

ARKADY. Would you go and meet him, Uncle Pavel?

PAVEL. (*to ARKADY:*) See? Still the message-boy. *Plus ça change . . .* (*PAVEL goes off and PROKO-FYICH is about to follow him.*)

NIKOLAI. And isn't Prokofyich looking well?

ARKADY. Prokofyich never changes. Thank you for picking us up.

PROKOFYICH. My pleasure. We'll go out looking for birds' nests tomorrow morning.

ARKADY. First thing. We'll show Bazarov all the good spots.

PROKOFYICH. Maybe you and I should go by ourselves first and then we —

PAVEL. (*off*) Prokofyich!

PROKOFYICH. Coming, sir. (*to ARKADY:*) It's good to have you back, Arkady.

ARKADY. Thank you. (*PROKOFYICH Exits* L.) Bird-nesting! He thinks I'm still a schoolboy.

NIKOLAI. In a way so do I.

ARKADY. And I deliberately mentioned Bazarov because they didn't get on very well on the journey. Prokofyich prefers the old ways, the old formalities. (*embraces the father again*) It's great to see you, Father.

NIKOLAI. Thank you.

ARKADY. And you're looking very fresh.

NIKOLAI. Fresh? At my age?

ARKADY. And so is Uncle Pavel. What's he doing with himself these days?

NIKOLAI. Oh, you know Pavel—killing time, as he says himself—walking—reading—(*whispers*) going to his English tailor and his French barber—thinking his own very secret thoughts . . . (*after a quick look round*) Arkady, there's one little matter before the others join us—I'm really a bit embarrassed mentioning it—

ARKADY. It's about Fenichka.

NIKOLAI. Shhh. How did you know?

ARKADY. Intuition.

NIKOLAI. Yes, it's about Fenichka. You know Fenichka, don't you? What am I talking about—of course you do! Well, as you know, Arkady, I've been very fond of her for a long time now. Her mother was the best housekeeper we ever had here and Fenichka has taken on those responsibilities with great assurance and skill, considering she's only twenty-three, just a year older than yourself; so I'm old enough to be her father, too, amn't I? Ha-ha. Anyhow, as I say, I've been very attached to her for a long time now; and indeed I have asked her—I have insisted—that she move out of that damp flat above the laundry and come into the main house. And I mention this now, Arkady, partly because I—I—because she's afraid you might . . . well, disapprove of her.

ARKADY. I might disapprove of Fenichka?

NIKOLAI. I hope you don't mind too much, Arkady.

ARKADY. Mind? Why in God's name should I mind?

NIKOLAI. Well, because . . . well, I just thought that . . . Anyhow, anyhow, the real reason I brought her into the house—and I want you to know that I do, I do care very much for the girl, Arkady—I thought it only proper and correct that she ought to be in the house after—(*pause*)—she'd had the baby.

ARKADY. Baby?

NIKOLAI. Hers and mine.

ARKADY. You mean—?

NIKOLAI. A boy.

ARKADY. You and—?

NIKOLAI. Six months old.

ARKADY. I have a new brother.

NIKOLAI. Half-brother.

ARKADY. Half-brother.

NIKOLAI. Mitya.

ARKADY. Mitya!

NIKOLAI. Mitya. Now you know it all. Actually he's the image of me. (*ARKADY suddenly laughs, throws his arms around his father.*)

ARKADY. Father, that is the best news ever!

NIKOLAI. Is it?

ARKADY. Of course it is! You're a sly old rascal but I think you're great. Congratulations!

NIKOLAI. You're not angry?

ARKADY. Angry? For God's sake, Father, I'm delighted for you!

NIKOLAI. Thank you, son. Thank you. We'll not talk about it before Pavel. I'm not sure he quite approves of the whole thing. You know Pavel with his silly notions of class and public decorum. (*PAVEL and BAZAROV Enter L.*) We can talk later.

(*BAZAROV, a student, dark, lean, intense. He senses*

that he is an outsider politically and socially in this house—hence the arrogance and curt manner.)

ARKADY. There he is! Come on, Bazarov! Come over here. Uncle Pavel you've obviously met—Pavel Petrovich Kirsanov. And this is my father, Nikolai Petrovich Kirsanov. Yevgeny Vassilyich Bazarov. (*BAZAROV bows formally.*)

NIKOLAI. You are most welcome to this house, Yevgeny Vassilyich. I hope you can stay with us for most of the summer and I hope you don't find us very dull company.

PAVEL. Do you remember a Doctor Bazarov in Father's old division? That's his father, he tells me.

NIKOLAI. Really? My goodness, it's a small . . . it's a . . .

PAVEL. Extraordinaire, n'est ce pas?

NIKOLAI. Indeed. And you're going to be a doctor, too? Great. Splendid. Sit down. Sit down. You must be tired after your journey.

BAZAROV. I'd prefer to stand.

NIKOLAI. Of course. Stand. Naturally. Stretch your legs. By all means—stand . . . Now to organize our lives. Let's have tea out here. Then you young men can have a rest and we'll eat about seven o'clock. All right? Piotr! He deliberately hides on me, you know. It's gone far beyond a joke. Dunyasha! Oh, you've no idea how difficult things are becoming. I'm not exaggerating, Pavel, am I? The old system—of course it had its failings. But now?—now I give all my land to the peasants to farm—*give* it to them. Will they even farm it for themselves? I wish you'd take an interest in it all, Arkady. It's becoming too much for me at my time of— sorry. (*to DUNYASHA:*) Ah, Dunyasha. Bring the samovar out here.

PAVEL. Cocoa for me, *s'il vous plaît*.

NIKOLAI. And a bottle of that black sherry in the sideboard. The young men may wish to — to — to dissipate! (*DUNYASHA is staring at BAZAROV.*)

ARKADY. Do you wish to dissipate, Bazarov? We would love to dissipate, Father.

NIKOLAI. Dunyasha!

DUNYASHA. Sorry, sir?

NIKOLAI. Black sherry. In the sideboard. And glasses. (*She goes into the house.*) What's the matter with that girl? And how is your father, Yevgeny Vassilyich? (*BAZAROV looks blankly at him. Pause.*) Your father — is he well?

BAZAROV. I suppose so. I haven't seen him for three years.

NIKOLAI. He has been away — has he? — traveling?

BAZAROV. Not that I know of.

NIKOLAI. Ah.

BAZAROV. I haven't seen him for three years because I haven't been home since I went to the university. (*silence*)

ARKADY. (*quickly*) Let me tell you about this character. He won the gold medal for oratory again this year — the third year in succession.

NIKOLAI. Wonderful!

ARKADY. And he is also — (*to BAZAROV:*) — no, don't try to stop me — he is also president of the philosophical society and editor of the magazine. It's an astonishing radical publication — the college authorities banned both issues this year! We were brought before the disciplinary council — remember? 'Revolutionaries! Damned revolutionaries!'

NIKOLAI. Oratory is an excellent discipline; excellent. I approve very strongly of — of — of — of oratory.

PAVEL. On what you do . . . orate?

BAZAROV. Politics. Philosophy.

PAVEL. They have something in common, have they?

ARKADY. Come on, Uncle Pavel. You know they have.

PAVEL. (*to BAZAROV:*) And your philosophy is?

ARKADY. Nihilism.

PAVEL. Sorry?

ARKADY. Nihilism, Uncle Pavel. Bazarov is a Nihilist. So am I.

NIKOLAI. Interesting word that. I imagine it comes from the Latin — *nihil* — nothing. Does it mean somebody who respects nothing? No, it doesn't.

ARKADY. Someone who looks at everything critically.

PAVEL. If there's a difference.

ARKADY. There's a significant difference, Pavel. Don't be so precious.

PAVEL. Me? — precious? Good Lord.

ARKADY. Nihilism begins by questioning all received ideas and principles no matter how venerated those ideas and principles are. And that leads to the inevitable conclusion that the world must be made anew. (*to BAZAROV:*) That's a fairly accurate summary of our stance, isn't it? (*BAZAROV shrugs indifferently and spreads his hands.*)

PAVEL. So you believe only in science?

ARKADY. We don't *believe* in anything. You can't believe in science any more than you can believe in the weather or farming or swimming.

NIKOLAI. I can tell you farming isn't what it used to be. In the past five years, the advances I've seen in farming techniques —

ARKADY. I wish you would stop trying to divert me with your juvenile asides, Father.

NIKOLAI. I am sorry.

PAVEL. A simple question: if you reject all accepted principles and all accepted precepts, what basis of conduct have you?

ARKADY. I don't understand what the simple question means.

PAVEL. On what basis do you conduct your life?

ARKADY. If something is useful — keep it. If it is not useful — out it goes. And the most useful thing we can do is repudiate, renounce, reject.

PAVEL. Everything?

ARKADY. Everything without use.

PAVEL. All accepted conventions, all art, all science?

ARKADY. What use are they? Out.

PAVEL. Civilization has just been disposed of, Nikolai.

NIKOLAI. But surely, Arkady, surely rejection means destruction; and surely we must construct, too?

ARKADY. Our first priority is to make a complete clearance. At this point in our evolution we have no right to indulge in the gratification of our own personal whims.

NIKOLAI. I don't think I had whims in mind, Arkady.

ARKADY. At times it's difficult to know what you have in mind, Father.

PAVEL. And when do you begin to preach this gospel publicly?

ARKADY. We're activists. We aren't preachers, are we, Bazarov? We are not going to —

PAVEL. Aren't you preaching now? (to NIKOLAI:) This is all nonsense; weary old materialistic nonsense I've heard a hundred times.

ARKADY. We know there is starvation and poverty; we know our politicians take bribes; we know the legal system is corrupt. We know all that. And we are tired listening to the 'liberals' and the 'progressives' —

PAVEL. So you have identified all society's evils —
NIKOLAI. Let him finish, Pavel.
PAVEL. I would prefer Yevgeny Vassilyich would do his own talking. (*to ARKADY:*) But you intend to do nothing constructive yourselves?
BAZAROV. We intend to do nothing constructive ourselves.
PAVEL. Just abuse people who do.
BAZAROV. Just abuse people who do.
PAVEL. And that's called Nihilism.
BAZAROV. And that's called Nihilism. Is this riveting discussion nearly over?
PAVEL. *Incroyable*! Let me see have I got it right —
NIKOLAI. I'm sure you've got it right, Pavel. Let's leave it for now.
PAVEL. First our saviours will demolish the country and then they will remake the country. But suppose some simple person were to suggest that our saviours were just bletherskites — gold-medal bletherskites?
BAZAROV. My grandfather was a serf, Pavel Petrovich. I believe I have some knowledge of the Russian people.
PAVEL. I'm sure you have a very —
BAZAROV. Indeed I believe I have at least as accurate and as sympathetic an understanding of their needs and of their mute aspirations as those absurd provincial aristocrats who affect English clothes and English customs; who believe they are civilized just because they speak cliché French; who talk endlessly about Mother Russia but who sit on their backsides and do sweet nothing for the '*bien public*' as they call it.
PAVEL. I suspect you're deliberately trying to —
BAZAROV. Words that come so easily to lips like yours — liberalism, progress, principles, civilization — they have no meaning in Russia. They are imported

words. Russia doesn't need them. But what Russia does need—and action will provide it, Pavel Petrovich, action, not words—what Russia does need is bread in the mouth. But before you can put bread in the mouth, you have got to plough the land—deep.

NIKOLAI. He's right, you know: ploughing is a very important part of the farming cycle. (*to ARKADY:*) Sorry. I didn't—

PAVEL. So the two of you are going to reform Russia.

BAZAROV. Remake Russia. Yes.

PAVEL. By force?

BAZAROV. (*shrugs*) If necessary.

ARKADY. All that's needed is a few people with total dedication. It was a penny candle that burned Moscow down, Uncle Pavel.

NIKOLAI. That's quite true, you know.

PAVEL. For God's sake, Nikolai, you know nothing about it!

NIKOLAI. I beg your pardon, Pavel—it *was* a penny candle burned Moscow down. That is an historical fact. Father was able to quote chapter and verse on it. (*to FENICHKA and DUNYASHA who have entered with a tray and samovar:*) Ah! Fenichka! Good! Great! Splendid! And beautifully timed—just when we had all come to a close understanding of one another's position. Have you the sherry? Excellent. (*to DUNYASHA:*) Just leave the tray there. Thank you. Thank you. You haven't met Arkady's friend, have you, Fenichka? Yevgeny Vassilyich Bazarov.

BAZAROV. Pleased to meet you.

FENICHKA. You're welcome.

BAZAROV. Thank you.

ARKADY. Dr Bazarov—almost.

FENICHKA. Welcome, Doctor.

NIKOLAI. (*to DUNYASHA who is staring at BAZAROV:*) Dunyasha, will you put the tray down on the seat, please?

DUNYASHA. Oh yes—yes, yes, yes.

NIKOLAI. I think this is yours, Pavel (*cocoa*).

PAVEL. Thanks. (*As the cups are being passed round ARKADY has a private word with FENICHKA.*)

ARKADY. Congratulations. (*she looks puzzled*) On the baby.

FENICHKA. Oh. (*She looks quickly towards NIKOLAI.*)

ARKADY. He's just told me.

FENICHKA. He wasn't sure how you'd react.

ARKADY. I'm pleased for you both.

FENICHKA. Thank you. (*NIKOLAI is aware of this private conversation.*)

NIKOLAI. You're sitting with us, Fenichka, aren't you?

FENICHKA. Not just now. I've got to bath Mitya and put him to bed. I'll join you later.

NIKOLAI. Please do. (*FENICHKA leaves.*)

DUNYASHA. Can I get you anything else?

NIKOLAI. That's everything, I think, Dunyasha. (*She is gazing at BAZAROV and does not move.*) Thank you. (*she goes*) There's something the matter with that girl today. Now to organize our lives. Let me tell you what plans we have in store for you. The first formal engagement is on Monday week. It's a rather long and convoluted story that—

PAVEL. It's quite simple: he's having a welcome-home party for you.

ARKADY. Great.

NIKOLAI. Some weeks ago quite out of the blue I had a visit from a young lady called Anna Sergeyevna Odintsov. (*to BAZAROV:*) An unusual name, isn't it?—Odintsov. Are you familiar with it?

BAZAROV. (*not listening*) No.

NIKOLAI. It was unknown to me, too, I must confess. Anyhow it transpires that the young lady's mother, may she rest in peace, and my good wife, may she rest in peace, were very close friends when they were young girls. But, as so often happens, they lost touch with one another shortly after they got married. But to cut a long story short. Anna Sergeyevna was rummaging in an attic in her home—

PAVEL. Could I have sugar?

NIKOLAI. —and she came across a bundle of letters written by your good mother, Maria, to her old friend— well, her young friend then. And Anna Sergeyevna had the kind thought that I might like to have these letters since they contain many references to myself. (*to BAZAROV:*) Arkady's mother and I were, as we say, walking out at the time.

BAZAROV. (*not listening*) Yes?

PAVEL. Cream, please.

NIKOLAI. I'd be delighted to have the letters, I said. So the following week Anna Sergeyevna Odintsov called on us again and handed over Maria's epistles and spent a very agreeable couple of hours with us—didn't she, Pavel?

PAVEL. I found her very . . . measured.

NIKOLAI. Did you think so?

PAVEL. And emotionally dehydrated.

ARKADY. Uncle Pavel!

PAVEL. Oh yes.

NIKOLAI. Well, I liked her very much.

ARKADY. What age is she?

NIKOLAI. I'm very bad at that sort of thing. I would imagine she might—

PAVEL. Twenty-nine.

ARKADY. Interesting.

NIKOLAI. Oh yes, an interesting lady.

PAVEL. Enormously wealthy. With a huge estate. And a widow.

ARKADY. *Very* interesting.

NIKOLAI. Very —? Oh, I see what you mean now. Very good. Very good. What else do we know about her? She lives with an eccentric old aunt, Princess Something-or-other.

PAVEL. Olga.

NIKOLAI. Olga. And she has a young sister called — what's the young sister's name?

PAVEL. Katerina.

NIKOLAI. That's it — Katya. All three are coming on Monday week. (*pause*) And we'll have a wonderful party. (*pause*) And we'll all have a wonderful time. (*pause*) Won't we?

PAVEL. If you'll excuse me. I get a headache when I sit too long in the sun.

NIKOLAI. We have a meeting with the new estate manager in half an hour, Pavel.

PAVEL. I'll be in my room.

NIKOLAI. I'll join you in a few minutes. (*As he Exits PAVEL puts his hand on ARKADY's shoulder and pats it. Then he leaves.*) Nothing Pavel likes better than a vigorous discussion, plenty of thrust and parry. We're inclined to go to seed here in the wilds, Yevgeny.

BAZAROV. Yes.

ARKADY. (*quickly*) What were the letters like?

NIKOLAI. Letters?

ARKADY. The letters Mother wrote to her friend about you.

NIKOLAI. Oh, they were . . . oh-ho, I'm afraid they were a bit naughty in places . . . very naughty in fact . . . in fact a few of them were very naughty indeed . . . You never really know what people are like, do you? We all have our codes. We all have our masks.

(*PIOTR Enters* L. *He is nineteen, exceedingly cocky and self-assured. He knows NIKOLAI is fond of him and he plays on that. He wears a single ear-ring and his hair is done in various vivid colours.*)

PIOTR. You wanted me, sir?
NIKOLAI. Yes, Piotr?
PIOTR. You sent for me, sir.
NIKOLAI. I did?
PIOTR. Dunyasha said you wanted me.
NIKOLAI. I'm sure I did, Piotr; and I'm sure you didn't hear me. (*to BAZAROV:*) Piotr's hearing is erratic.
PIOTR. (*aggrieved*) My hearing is perfect, sir. I was slaving in the stables. You could scream and I wouldn't hear you there, sir.
NIKOLAI. Never mind now, Piotr. Look who's here.
PIOTR. I know. I saw the carriage. Welcome home, Arkady.
ARKADY. Thank you, Piotr.
NIKOLAI. And this is another young graduate — well, almost a graduate — Yevgeny Vassilyich.
PIOTR. Sir.
BAZAROV. Hello.
NIKOLAI. Do you like his multicoloured hair?
ARKADY. It's what all the young dudes in Petersburg are wearing, Piotr.
PIOTR. I know that. But nobody around this place does.
NIKOLAI. And his single blue ear-ring?
PIOTR. Pardon me, sir — turquoise.
NIKOLAI. Forgive me, Piotr — turquoise. I beg your

pardon. (*waving him away*) No, I don't want you now. Yes, I do. Take this tray away with you. And get the carriage out and bring it round to the back.

PIOTR. Certainly, sir. No sooner said.

NIKOLAI. 'No sooner said'! He has my heart broken. (*PIOTR Exits.*) And I'm very fond of him — he's so cheeky. (*Looks at watch.*) Five thirty. I must run. Show Yevgeny where the guest-room is. Have a wash. Walk around. Take a rest. Do whatever pleases you. We'll eat at seven. And welcome again — both of you.

(*He leaves. ARKADY is annoyed with his friend: he thinks his exchange with PAVEL was too personal. BAZAROV is unaware of this. He goes to the samovar.*)

BAZAROV. How did your father get that limp?

ARKADY. Broken leg when he was young. Badly set.

BAZAROV. I like him. He's a decent man. An astute bird, too. What's the relationship between him and the blonde woman?

ARKADY. Fenichka. She's his mistress.

BAZAROV. Ah. I got a whiff of something there.

ARKADY. I suppose that's one way of putting it.

BAZAROV. Have they known each other long?

ARKADY. She has a child by him.

BAZAROV. Good-looking woman. A nice self-awareness about her. Fenichka.

ARKADY. He should marry her.

BAZAROV. Who needs marriage? Your father's a lot more progressive than you, my friend. I suspect — just glancing round the yard — I suspect he's not the most organized landowner in Russia. But his heart's in the right place. Tea?

ARKADY. I thought you were a bit severe on Uncle Pavel.

BAZAROV. God, what a freak that is!

ARKADY. It sounded like a personal attack — cliché French — all that stuff.

BAZAROV. Have you any idea of the shock it is to walk into a place like this, miles from anywhere, and to be confronted by that — that decaying dandy? And all those archaic theories about 'civilization' and a 'basis of conduct'! He's a bloody absurdity!

ARKADY. He was considered to be the most handsome officer in the army in his day; and the best gymnast.

BAZAROV. No, he's not absurd — he's grotesque.

ARKADY. He was made a captain when he was only twenty-one. Women just threw themselves at him. And he has travelled everywhere and read everything. And he speaks three or four languages. And he dined once with Louis Philippe; and he and the Duke of Wellington corresponded on and off for years.

BAZAROV. (*imitating PAVEL*) Good heavens.

ARKADY. And then, when he was in his mid-twenties, he fell in love — one of those passions that consumes totally. I remember hearing the story when I was very young. She was a princess; married; with a child.

(*DUNYASHA appears on the veranda and shakes out a tablecloth. BAZAROV pretends to think she is waving at him and waves back at her. DUNYASHA withdraws coyly.*)

BAZAROV. That Dunyasha lady has a sporty eye.

ARKADY. And she had this radiant golden hair and when she let it down 'it fell to below her knees', like Rapunzel in the fairy story. They lived together for a while. Then she got tired of him. Cleared off to Germany, France, somewhere. Just disappeared. He followed her, of course; pursued her frantically for ten years all over Europe. Then he got word that she had died, apparently in some kind of demented state, in some shabby boarding-house in Paris.

BAZAROV. Where else.

ARKADY. Oh yes, there was another detail.

BAZAROV. (*pretended eagerness*) What was that?

ARKADY. Early in their affair he gave her a ring with a sphinx engraved on the stone. And the family legend has it that she said to him, 'Why the sphinx?'

BAZAROV. 'You are that sphinx.'

ARKADY. That's right! That's what he said! And exactly seven weeks after she died a package was delivered to his club. He opened it up and inside —

BAZAROV. — was the ring.

ARKADY. Yes. That was in 1848, the year Mother died. Father was alone here then, lost without his Maria. He asked Uncle Pavel to join him. And he came. And he has lived here, really like a recluse, ever since, in a sort of profound and perpetual melancholy . . . I'm very fond of him. I think he's a good man, Uncle Pavel. (*pause*)

BAZAROV. You astonish me at times, Arkady. I tell myself that you *are* maturing politically, intellectually, emotionally. And then you come out with the greatest load of romantic hogwash that quite honestly alarms me. Rapunzel — radiant golden hair — passions that consume totally —

ARKADY. If you knew Pavel as well as I —

BAZAROV. Look at him dispassionately. The shape and character of his entire life was determined by a single, ridiculous passion. And when that ridiculous passion wasn't reciprocated — what happens? He sinks into a 'profound and perpetual melancholy'! For the rest of his life! Because of a crazy woman! That's the behaviour of an imbecile! (*beginning to win ARKADY over*) Let me give you Dr Bazarov's Principles Concerning the Proper Ordering of the Relationships between Men and Women.

ARKADY. I must write these deathless words down.

BAZAROV. One. Romantic love is a fiction. Two. There is nothing at all mysterious between the sexes. The relationship is quite simply physical. Three. To believe that the relationship should be dressed up in the trappings of chivalry is crazy. The troubadours were all lunatics. Four. If you fancy a woman, any woman, always, always try to make love to her. If you want to dissipate, dissipate.

ARKADY. Poor old Father—I was a bit sharp with him.

BAZAROV. And if you can't make love to that particular woman, so what? Believe Dr Bazarov—there are plenty more fish in the sea.

ARKADY. You're a bastard, Bazarov. You know that?

BAZAROV. Admit it. Am I not right?

ARKADY. (*thawing*) A perverse bastard—that's what you are.

BAZAROV. Draw up a list of all the women you'd like to make love to—no commitment, no responsibilities —just for the sheer pleasure of it.

ARKADY. Keep your voice down, man.

BAZAROV. No complications of 'love', romance, none of that rubbish.

ARKADY. That's a game for undergraduates. I'm a graduate—remember?

BAZAROV. A quick roll in the hay—great fun—goodbye.

ARKADY. All gross pigs, you medicals.

BAZAROV. I'll start you off. Natasha Petrova.

ARKADY. Natasha who?

BAZAROV. The inconstancy of the man! Your first year in Petersburg—the landlady's big red-headed daughter—Natasha the Greyhound!

ARKADY. Come on, Bazarov. There was nothing at all to that.

BAZAROV. You wrote a sonnet to her.

ARKADY. I never did!

BAZAROV. 'Could I outstrip the beauty of that form That haunts these dark and wretched hours called life—'

ARKADY. All right—all right! That was just a passing—

BAZAROV. Exactly. Quick roll—great fun—goodbye. She's number one. Dunyasha?

ARKADY. Dunyasha?—here?

BAZAROV. On the list or not?

ARKADY. I never really thought about her in that—

BAZAROV. A sporty eye, an open heart, a great armful.

ARKADY. Now that you mention her, I suppose she—

BAZAROV. She's elected; number two. Anna Sergeyevna?

ARKADY. Who's she?

BAZAROV. The woman who's coming for the party on Monday week.

ARKADY. We've never seen her.

BAZAROV. Who cares?

ARKADY. She's wealthy.

BAZAROV. Twenty-nine years of age.

ARKADY. A huge estate.

BAZAROV. And a widow.

ARKADY. Is that important?

BAZAROV. The experience, man.

ARKADY. Good point. What do you say?

BAZAROV. If only for the experience — number three. And her young sister — Katya?

ARKADY. I think so.

BAZAROV. Vote. Yes or no.

ARKADY. Katya? I like Katya. I fancy Katya. Yes.

BAZAROV. Elected. Good. Four so far. (*FENICHKA appears on the veranda.*)

FENICHKA. Yevgeny Vassilyich!

BAZAROV. Hello.

FENICHKA. The baby has some kind of a rash on the back of his neck. Would you take a look at it for me?

BAZAROV. It would be a pleasure. Where is he?

FENICHKA. He's back here in the kitchen.

BAZAROV. I'm on my way. (*to ARKADY:*) My first professional job.

ARKADY. I'd be sure to get a second opinion, Fenichka.

BAZAROV. (*softly*) Would you say that Fenichka is a possible number five?

ARKADY. Bazarov, you — !

BAZAROV. In jest, my friend, in jest. (*He goes towards the veranda where FENICHKA is waiting for him.*)

ARKADY. (*calls*) Even in jest! Bazarov, for God's sake, man. (*BAZAROV turns at the steps and smiles back at him. Then he and FENICHKA go into the house.*)

SCENE 2

Early June. After dinner.
NIKOLAI and KATYA are playing duets on the piano in
*   the living-room. KATYA is eighteen, open, spirited,*
*   garrulous. FENICHKA is standing beside the piano*

*turning the pages on NIKOLAI's instructions.
BAZAROV is outside on the veranda, leaning across
the rail, slowly eating a dish of ice-cream. PAVEL is
sitting alone and remote* D.S.R.; *reading. ANNA is
sitting* D.S.L., *listening to the music. She is an ele-
gant, carefully groomed, circumspect woman. She
deliberately lives within certain emotional limits and
is wary of any intrusion inside them or any excursion
outside them. The PRINCESS is sitting* U.S.R., *be-
neath an enormous parasol which partly conceals
her. Now and then she emerges from behind it. She is
very old, very eccentric, very energetic. She con-
stantly and vigorously masticates imaginary food
and every so often brushes imaginary crumbs from
her sleeve and skirt.
Just before the music comes to an end NIKOLAI calls:*

NIKOLAI. Wonderful, Katya. Terrific. Don't stop.
Let's do it again from the beginning. Splendid.
Two-and-three-and—

(*They begin the piece again and keep playing throughout
the early part of the scene. ARKADY rushes through
the living-room and out into the garden, carrying a
dish of ice-cream. He is very elated.*)

ARKADY. (*as he passes behind BAZAROV*) Get your-
self some more ice-cream before it all melts. (*He leaps
down the steps.*)
BAZAROV. (*as ARKADY crosses before him*) I think
the dehydrated widow fancies you.
ARKADY. Doing well, amn't I?
BAZAROV. Give her a message for me.
ARKADY. What?

BAZAROV. Tell her I'd like to do my anatomy practical on her.

ARKADY. Cut that out, Bazarov.

BAZAROV. I'm sure she'd agree. (*ARKADY crosses over to the PRINCESS.*)

ARKADY. Can I get you anything, Princess Olga?

PRINCESS. (*emerging*) Cat.

ARKADY. Sorry?

PRINCESS. I smell cat.

ARKADY. Cat?

PRINCESS. Cat-cat-cat. Damn place must be overrun with them. Shoot them all! Shoot them! Shoot them! They'll overrun you if you don't. My father told me that. (*She vanishes behind the parasol. He goes to ANNA.*)

ANNA. It's best to pay no attention to her.

ARKADY. She sounds so furious.

ANNA. Ignore her. She lives quite contentedly in her own world.

ARKADY. There you are. (*offers ice-cream*) I'm afraid it's gone a bit soft.

ANNA. You have it.

ARKADY. I've had enough. Go ahead. There's plenty more. Loads of it. We eat it all the time here. In the summer. God, she's really a magnificent pianist, Katya.

ANNA. She's very competent; no more than that.

ARKADY. And she can sight-read brilliantly. I love that piece. I remember Father and Mother playing it together when I was very small. I'm sure you play, too?

ANNA. No.

ARKADY. Yes, you do. You're being modest.

ANNA. I don't, Arkady.

ARKADY. I'm sure you're a brilliant pianist.

ANNA. No.

ARKADY. I don't believe you. And I'm told you're a

painter. (*She shakes her head.*) Yes, you are. Katya told me. She says you're terrific with water-colours.

ANNA. Katerina exaggerates.

ARKADY. Bazarov and I are going to visit his parents soon, maybe at the end of next week. I was wondering if we could call on you on our way there?

ANNA. We'd be glad to see you.

ARKADY. Great! Tomorrow, maybe? Are you sure that's all right?

ANNA. He looks like a painter. Is he artistic?

ARKADY. Uncle Pavel?

ANNA. Your friend — who believes in nothing.

ARKADY. Bazarov? He's a total philistine! (*calls*) We're talking about you! (*BAZAROV points to his ears, points into the living-room; he cannot hear above the music. Shouts.*) Anna Sergeyevna wants to know — (*he gives up*) It doesn't matter.

ANNA. (*beckons*) Come and join us.

ARKADY. Keep him off politics or he'll give you a boring lecture. I'm a Nihilist, too, you know; like Bazarov.

ANNA. (*watching BAZAROV approach*) Really?

ARKADY. We've a very active cell in Petersburg. There aren't all that many of us but we're absolutely, totally dedicated. Anna wants to know if you're artistic!

ANNA. Arkady says you're a philistine.

ARKADY. He's the worst kind of philistine — he's a scientist.

BAZAROV. What is art for?

ARKADY. (*to ANNA:*) I told you.

BAZAROV. Is it necessary?

(*ANNA's attention has switched to BAZAROV. In an attempt to hold her ARKADY launches into his*

monologue. While he lectures, ANNA and BA-
ZAROV conduct a mute dialogue; 'Sit here' — 'No,
thanks' — 'There's a stool' — 'I'd prefer to stand' —
'There's a chair' — 'I'm fine' — etc.)

ARKADY. And the answer to that is: What does the
word necessary mean in that context? Is that dish
necessary? — that tree? — that cloud formation? We're
not exactly in unison on this issue, Bazarov and I. He
believes that Nihilism and art are seldom compatible. I
don't. But I believe that at this point in our history and in
our sociological development it would be wrong for us
now to channel our depleted energies into artistic endea-
vour, not because there is anything intrinsically wrong,
or indeed right, with artistic endeavour — but I believe
that whatever energies we can muster now have got to be
poured into the primary and enormous task of remaking
an entire society and that imperative is not only a social
obligation but perhaps even a moral obligation and in-
deed it is not improbable that the execution of that task
may even have elements of . . . of artistic pur-
suit . . . or so it seems to me . . . (*He tails off in some
confusion, unsure that he has made his point, any point,
unsure that he has impressed ANNA, unsure that she has
even listened to him. Pause.*)
PRINCESS. (*suddenly emerging*) My father always said
that the quickest and most efficient way to break in a
difficult young horse was to hit him over the head with a
crow-bar. (*She demonstrates.*) Bang between the ears!
Ha-ha. He was right, you know. I've done it myself. And
it works! It works! It works! (*She vanishes again. Pause.*)
BAZAROV. Lively music, isn't it?
ANNA. So you're not a total philistine. (*BAZAROV
shrugs.*)

BAZAROV. Silly word.

ARKADY. What word?

BAZAROV. Philistine.

ARKADY. No, it's not. It's a precise word.

ANNA. Art can at least help us to know and understand people, can't it?

BAZAROV. Living does that. (*laying down ice-cream dish*) That was good.

ANNA. Not to the same extent; not in any depth.

(*DUNYASHA Enters and picks up various dishes around the lawn.*)

BAZAROV. What is there to understand in depth? All men are similar physically and intellectually. Each has a brain, a spleen, heart, lungs. Intellectually? — darker and lighter shadings, that's all. We're like trees in the forest. Ask any botanist. Know one birch, know them all. (*DUNYASHA is about to pick up the dish beside ANNA.*)

ANNA. I'm not finished yet.

DUNYASHA. Sorry, Miss.

BAZAROV. And Dunyasha is the most wholesome and uncomplicated birch-tree in the whole of Russia.

DUNYASHA. What does that mean?

BAZAROV. It means that you're beautiful and desirable.

ARKADY. Don't listen to him, Dunyasha. Uncle Pavel says he's a bletherskite. (*DUNYASHA loves this. She gives a great whoop of laughter.*)

DUNYASHA. He did not, did he? A bletherskite! That's great! That's what he is all right! (*She goes off laughing.*)

BAZAROV. (*calls*) I still think you're beautiful.

ANNA. So there is no difference between a stupid person and an intelligent person, between a good person and a bad person?

BAZAROV. Of course there is, just as there is a difference between a sick person and a healthy person. The man with tuberculosis has the same *kind* of lungs as you and I but they are in a different condition; and as medicine advances we know how to correct that condition. Moral disease, moral imbalance has different causes — our educational system, religious superstition, heredity, the polluted moral atmosphere our society breathes. But remake society and you eradicate *all* disease.

ANNA. Physical and moral?

BAZAROV. All.

ANNA. (*to ARKADY:*) Does he believe that? (*to BAZAROV:*) That if you reform society —

BAZAROV. Remake.

ANNA. Then all illness, all evil, all stupidity disappear?

BAZAROV. Because in our remade society the words stupid and clever, good and bad, will have lost the meaning you invest them with, will probably come to have no meaning at all. Do they not play polkas in the houses of the gentry?

ANNA. (*to ARKADY:*) What do you think?

ARKADY. I agree with Bazarov. Bazarov's right. (*ANNA looks keenly at BAZAROV.*)

ANNA. (*Suddenly to ARKADY:*) Could I have some more of that ice-cream?

ARKADY. (*He jumps to his feet, eager to serve.*) Wonderful, isn't it? I made it myself. Ice-cream, Uncle Pavel?

PAVEL. What's that?

ARKADY. Ice-cream — do you want some?

BAZAROV. 'Good heavens, no'.

PAVEL. Good heavens, no.

ARKADY. (*coldly to BAZAROV:*) What about you?

BAZAROV. Not for me. (*ARKADY goes to the PRINCESS.*)

ARKADY. Princess, would you like—(*She emerges momentarily and scowls at him.*)

PRINCESS. Would I like what? What would I like?

ARKADY. Sorry. (*He flees. Trips on the veranda steps.*)

ANNA. He's such a nice young man.

BAZAROV. You have unbalanced him.)

ARKADY. (*calls above the piano music*) Anybody for ice-cream?

KATYA. Me, Arkady. Please.

ARKADY. Fenichka?

(*She signals no. He goes to her and dances her round the room in time to the music. ANNA claps.*)

ANNA. (*calls*) Very good, Arkady! Lovely!

BAZAROV. Exquisite.

ANNA. He's a very good dancer.

BAZAROV. (*sharply*) Altogether he's such a nice young man.

ANNA. (*calls*) Beautiful, Arkady. Very elegant.

ARKADY. Can't hear you.

BAZAROV. He can't take his eyes off you.

ANNA. Do you dance?

BAZAROV. No.

ANNA. I love dancing.

BAZAROV. Naturally. All aristocrats love dancing.

ANNA. I've told you, Yevgeny—I'm not an aristocrat. Tell me more about your Nihilism.

BAZAROV. It's not mine. I don't possess it like an estate. Tell me what you believe in.

ANNA. Routine; order; discipline.

BAZAROV. That's how you conduct your life, not what you believe in.

ANNA. It's adequate for me.

BAZAROV. Because you have no beliefs or because your beliefs have no passion?

ANNA. Passion is a luxury. I make no excursions outside what I know and can handle.

BAZAROV. These new psychiatrists would say that you avoid belief because belief demands commitment and you're afraid of commitment. And you're afraid of commitment because it would demand everything of you. And because you're not prepared to give everything, you give nothing. And you excuse yourself by calling passion a luxury but you know in your heart that your excuse is a lie.

ANNA. I'm not a liar, Yevgeny Vassilyich.

BAZAROV. I haven't met all that many aristocrats like you in my life—

ANNA. I am not an—

BAZAROV. —but I've noticed that their brain is divided into two equal parts. One part is totally atrophied —the part that might be capable of generosity, enthusiasm, of a thirst for social change, of the desire for risk, for the big gamble, for that dangerous extreme. So they function, these aristocratic cripples, they function with the portion that is left to them; and like some mutilated organ it becomes unnaturally developed and unnaturally active. Hence your aristocrat's irrational obsession with wheat-yield and good-management and productivity and efficiency—

ANNA. And routine and order and discipline. Why are you being so difficult?

BAZAROV. Perhaps I haven't the grace for aristocratic ladies like you.

ANNA. My father, my handsome, gambling, risking, reckless father died when I was twenty. Katerina was only twelve. For two years we lived in penury, the kind of grinding poverty I suspect you have never known, Yevgeny. Then I met a man who was twenty-five years older than me. He was very wealthy, eccentric, a hypochondriac, enormously fat. He had no illusions about himself. He asked me to marry him. I thought about it very carefully and then I said yes. We had six years together. I still miss him. He was a kind man.

BAZAROV. So?

ANNA. So that's all. I suppose I'm trying to—Oh I don't know why I told you that.

BAZAROV. I'm afraid I'm lost here. I mean—am I to applaud your circumspection in netting a rich old eccentric—or commiserate with you on your bereavement?—or congratulate you on your sudden wealth?

ANNA. Let's not talk about it any more.

BAZAROV. Or are you just teasing my appetite for the full biography? Because if you are, I'm afraid I find it less than gripping. But it does have the markings of the kind of rags-to-riches novelette that someone like Dunyasha, or indeed the very nice young Arkady, would probably find irrestible. (*ANNA jumps to her feet and would leave but BAZAROV catches her by the arms.*) Oh my God, Anna—forgive me—I'm sorry—I'm sorry—please, please forgive me—(*The music has stopped. Everybody is aware of the scene, of the raised voices. Everybody is staring at them. BAZAROV realizes he is holding her and lets her go. Lowering his voice.*) I've no idea why I said that—it was unpardonable, unpardonable—I'm sorry—I'm deeply sorry—please forgive me—please. (*Silence. PAVEL, the only person unaware of the scene, closes his book and walks slowly across the stage towards ANNA.*)

PAVEL. (*applauding the pianists*) Bravo! Well done!

Lovely! Thank you. Your sister is a very talented pianist.

ANNA. What are you reading, Pavel Petrovich?

PAVEL. This? Ne vaut pas la peine d'être lu. *The Romance of the Forest* by an English novelist called Mrs Anna Ward Radcliffe. A simple lady. But it kills time. Harmlessly. (*As he goes into the living-room, ARKADY Enters carrying two dishes of ice-cream — one for KATYA and one for ANNA. With distaste.*) Good Lord.

ARKADY. Good Lord, it's lovely, Uncle Pavel. Here we are! Who ordered what? Katya — there you are — one vanilla ice-cream coated with chocolate dressing and topped with a single glistening cherry.

KATYA. Thank you, Arkady. Oh, lovely!

BAZAROV. (*softly to ANNA:*) Please forgive me. I'm deeply sorry. (*He exits quickly L.*)

ARKADY. (*to KATYA:*) My great pleasure. (*coming outside*) And one without dressing for Anna Sergeyevna Odintsov. (*KATYA comes down beside him.*)

KATYA. Did you really make it yourself?

ARKADY. Why the surprise? I'm expert at all foods, amn't I, Bazarov? Where's Bazarov? In the flat we shared I did all the cooking and he did all the washing and cleaning.

KATYA. (*to ANNA:*) You're pale. Are you all right?

ANNA. I'm fine — fine — we'll soon have to go, Katerina.

KATYA. No, we're not leaving for some time. I like it here. (*NIKOLAI and FENICHKA come down.*)

NIKOLAI. I really enjoyed that. I haven't played piano duets since Maria and I used to sit in there and — (*recovering*) — oh, not for years and years. Did we go on too long?

ANNA. Not long enough. We had a lovely evening.

NIKOLAI. I hope it's the first of many. It's beginning to

get cold. Do you think the Princess is warm enough?

ANNA. She's all right. Anyway it's time we got the carriage ready.

NIKOLAI. Piotr! Piotr! He must be somewhere around. Ah, Prokofyich, would you see to Madam Odintsov's carriage?

PROKOFYICH. Certainly, madam. (*ANNA pushes the parasol aside.*)

ANNA. Time to move, Auntie Olga. We have a long journey before us.

PRINCESS. Long journeys — short journeys — my father always said they all end up in the same place: nowhere, nowhere, nowhere.

(*ANNA takes her arm and together they go into the living-room. ARKADY watches ANNA as she goes.*)

KATYA. You were to show me the litter of pups, Arkady.

ARKADY. Sorry?

KATYA. The litter of pups — you were to show me them.

ARKADY. So I was. We'll go just now. They're in the stable.

KATYA. How many are there?

ARKADY. Four. Would you like one?

KATYA. What do you mean — would I like one? We talked about this all morning and you said I could have the pick of the litter. Don't you remember?

ARKADY. Of course I remember. And it's the pick of the litter you'll get, Katerina.

KATYA. Katya! Katya! Katya! We talked about that, too! I told you I loathe Katerina. Anna's the only one who calls me Katerina.

ARKADY. Sorry, Katya. The pick of the litter—your choice—whatever one you want. Or take two of them. Or three of them. Or take them all.

KATYA. 'Take them all'! You're an awful clown, you know.

ARKADY. Why?

KATYA. Just the way you go on. If you want my honest opinion, I think you're not a very mature person yet.

ARKADY. Really?!

KATYA. But that will come in time.

ARKADY. Oh, good. Then I'll be like you.

KATYA. No, no—always a little behind. But close enough. Come on—Anna wants to leave soon.

(*She leads him off* L. *NIKOLAI and FENICHKA move* D.S. *DUNYASHA comes into the living-room and tidies around. She is singing.*)

NIKOLAI. I wouldn't be at all surprised if Arkady has fallen for young Katya. I noticed, when we were playing the piano, she kept watching him.

FENICHKA. I think it's Anna Sergeyevna he likes.

NIKOLAI. Do you think so? Oh, I would hope not. Anna Sergeyevna is a splendid young woman but much too sophisticated for Arkady. Sit down beside me. You must be tired. You had a busy day.

FENICHKA. I was tired earlier but I'm fine now. When are the boys leaving?

NIKOLAI. The end of next week, I believe. And I'm glad—no, not that they're leaving—(*whispers*)—but that Bazarov is finally going to his parents. Hasn't seen them for three whole years! Can you imagine—not since he started college!

FENICHKA. Some people live like that. It doesn't mean he doesn't care for them.

NIKOLAI. That's true. Maybe it's just a matter of being alert to certain sensibilities. He's fond of you — Bazarov.

FENICHKA. Is he?

NIKOLAI. Oh, yes. He's more relaxed with you than with anybody else in the house.

FENICHKA. I like him, too. Strange man.

NIKOLAI. And Arkady's also fond of you, thank heaven!

FENICHKA. I've very fond of Arkady.

(*DUNYASHA Exits. They are alone.*)

NIKOLAI. And of Mitya. Calls him 'little half-brother'.

FENICHKA. I've heard him. It's funny to see them playing together.

NIKOLAI. We had a long talk the other day. We were alone in the garden here. It was like old times — just the two of us. And then do you know what he did out of the blue? He scolded me!

FENICHKA. Arkady?

NIKOLAI. Quite severely. He said I shouldn't have allowed you to live above that laundry for so long.

FENICHKA. (*becoming embarrassed*) What Arkady doesn't know is that the room above the laundry is the warmest room in the house.

NIKOLAI. It is also damp. Anyhow his point was that you were pregnant and you should have been in the main building; that it was most insensitive of me. And he's right.

FENICHKA. That's all over, Nikolai. I'm in the main house now. You're right — it is getting cold.

NIKOLAI. He said, too, that we should be married. Yes. He had no doubts whatever. He thinks it's ridiculous we're not married. Remarkable, isn't it?

FENICHKA. What it?

NIKOLAI. That this is his attitude. And I found it very reassuring. More than reassuring—encouraging, most encouraging. Wouldn't you agree?

FENICHKA. Oh, yes; most encouraging.

NIKOLAI. And of course Pavel would be in favour. No question about his attitude.

FENICHKA. Has he said that to you?

NIKOLAI. He doesn't have to say it—I know Pavel. Convention—decorum. Oh, yes, Pavel will want the properties observed. So, since I now know what Arkady thinks—and unlike his dithering old father he hadn't a moment's hesitation—and since I've always known that Pavel would be in favour—(*FENICHKA buries her face in her handkerchief and cries. NIKOLAI watches her in alarm and bewilderment.*) Fenichka? Fenichka, what's the matter with—? My God, what have I done wrong? Did I do anything?—did I say anything? Did somebody hurt you? Who hurt you? Please don't cry, Fenichka. Please. Tell me what's the matter with you. Fenichka? Fenichka? (*She continues to cry. He continues to watch her in bewilderment.*)

SCENE 3

End of June.
ARKADY and BAZAROV are sitting at the dining-room table in Bazarov's home. With them are Bazarov's father, VASSILY IVANYICH BAZAROV, and his mother, ARINA VLASSYEVNA. VASSILY IVAN-YICH is in his early sixties, a tall, thin, pipe-smoking man dressed in an old military jacket. He is very ill at ease in the presence of his guests and talks too

*much — and is aware that he is talking too much —
to hide his unease.*
*ARINA VLASSYEVNA is a small, plump woman in her
fifties. The first impression is of a quiet, simple coun-
try woman. But she is alert to every nuance in the
conversation and watches her son and his friend to
gauge their reaction to her husband's compulsive
talking. Two servants attend the table —
TIMOFEICH, an old retainer, almost decrepit, and
FEDKA, a very young boy who is employed only
because of the visitors. FEDKA is barefooted.*
Lunch has just finished.

VASSILY. Very good question, Arkady Nikolayevich:
how do I pass the time? Excellent question. And I will tell
you the answer to that question. Timofeich, more black-
currant tea for our guest.

ARKADY. Just a little. (*To ARINA*) That was a very
nice lunch. Thank you.

ARINA. You're welcome. (*BAZAROV gets to his feet
and paces around the room.*)

VASSILY. Yevgeny?

BAZAROV. None for me.

ARINA. (*privately to BAZAROV:*) Take another
biscuit.

BAZAROV. (*playfully shaking his head*) Shhh!

ARINA. I'm going to have to fatten you up over the
next two months.

(*BAZAROV responds by puffing out his cheeks and his
chest and miming a fat man.*)

VASSILY. How do I pass the time? I'm a bit like ancient
Gaul: I'm divided into *tres partes,* as our friend Caesar

might put it. One part is the reader. Another part is the gardener. And the third part is the practising doctor — even though I'm supposed to have retired years ago. Not a day passes but there's a patient at my door. (*to ARINA:*) That wouldn't be incorrect, my pet, would it? And interestingly enough all of those three parts add up to one complete integer. My reading is all medical reading. My gardening is all medical gardening — I believe I have the best garden of medicinal herbs in the whole province. That wouldn't be inaccurate, my pet, would it? Nature itself as healer — it's the answer, you know. As our friend Paracelsus puts it: I trust *in herbis, in verbis et in lapidibus.*

BAZAROV. (*to ARKADY:*) Father was a great classical scholar in his day.

VASSILY. Great? I wouldn't say I —

BAZAROV. Won a medal for Latin composition. Silver. When he was only twelve.

VASSILY. I suspect he's mocking me. Are you mocking me?

BAZAROV. Me?

ARINA. Finish your story, Vassily.

VASSILY. Where was I?

BAZAROV. *In herbis, in verbis et in lapidibus.*

VASSILY. Tending my garden, attending my patients, and in my spare time looking after my modest farm. (*to ARKADY:*) I shouldn't say 'my modest farm' — I'm a plebeian, a *homo novus* — Yevgeny's mother is the patrician.

ARINA. Vassily! (*BAZAROV bows to his mother and kisses her hand.*)

BAZAROV. Her serene highness, Arina Vlassyevna Bazarov.

ARINA. Behave yourself.

VASSILY. For God's sake, Fedka, will you put something on your feet. Timofeich, take this little urchin away and dress him correctly. Arkady Nikolayevich will think he's staying with some sort of primitives.

BAZAROV. Isn't that what we are?

VASSILY. You're very facetious today, young man. But where was I? Yes, talking of medicine. You'll enjoy this. I hear that a retired major about six miles from here is doing a bit of doctoring. So one day, when we meet at the market, this major and I, I said, 'I hear you're in practice, Major?' 'Yes,' he said. 'Where did you qualify?' 'I never qualified,' he said. 'Never? But where did you study your medicine?' 'I never studied medicine.' 'But you practice medicine, Major?' 'Oh, yes. But not for money—just for the good of the community.' (*VASSILY alone laughs at this. ARKADY smiles politely.*) I love that—'just for the good of the community'—I really love that. Wonderful man to have around in a typhus epidemic. Incidentally there's a lot of it around . . . typhus . . . (*pause*).

ARINA. (*to ARKADY:*) How long did you stay with this—this Madam Odintsov?

ARKADY. A week—(*to BAZAROV:*)—wasn't it? I've lost track of time.

BAZAROV. Eight nights.

ARINA. (*to ARKADY:*) And you had a nice time there?

ARKADY. It was sheer luxury. We were a bit overwhelmed at first, weren't we?

BAZAROV. Were we?

ARKADY. Well, I was.

BAZAROV. Yes, you were.

ARKADY. A butler in black tails, footmen in livery, scores of maids and servants all over the place. It's really a miniature empire she has there.

ARINA. And she lives with an old aunt and a young sister, this Madam Odintsov?

ARKADY. The old aunt's as mad as a hatter.

ARINA. And the young sister?

ARKADY. Katya is — (*to BAZAROV:*) — how would you describe Katya?

BAZAROV. You should have no difficulty. You voted her on your list.

ARINA. List? What list?

ARKADY. (*embarrassed*) Oh, we made a list, Yevgeny and I — a sort of silly list of — of — of all the pretty girls we know.

ARINA. Ah. And Katya is on that list?

ARKADY. She *was* on the list — at the beginning. She was on the first list.

ARINA. I see. She was pretty but she's not pretty now.

ARKADY. Oh, she's pretty, very pretty, isn't she?

BAZAROV. You're not alert to Mother's subtleties, Arkady. When she inquires about 'this — this Madam Odintsov', can't you hear the disapproval in her voice? She has already made up her mind that This Madam Odintsov is what novelists call an adventuress.

ARINA. That's not true.

BAZAROV. (*He hugs her affectionately and laughs.*) You're suspicious of her.

ARINA. Don't be silly, Yevgeny.

BAZAROV. You dislike her intensely.

ARINA. I never even heard of the woman until yesterday. He's trying to annoy me.

BAZAROV. In fact you hate The Woman. I know exactly what it means when that little nose twitches like that. It always gives you away.

ARINA. And you? What do you think of her? (*BAZAROV hugs her again and laughs.*)

BAZAROV. Oh no, no, no, no, no, no, no; you're not going to turn the tables like that, Arina Vlassyevna. Isn't she a cunning little squirrel?

VASSILY. (*to ARKADY:*) They're well met, the pair of them.

BAZAROV. The question you really want to ask, Mother—it has tormented you since we arrived yesterday—what you want to ask straight out is: Am I in love with This Madam Odintsov? And the answer is: I don't believe in love, in falling in love, in being in love. Arkady and I spent a pleasant week with Katya and Anna. They're good company. I'm fond of them both. And that's it—*finis fabulae*—(*to VASSILY:*)—correct?

VASSILY. Very good, Yevgeny.

BAZAROV. If there is such a thing as a *maladie d'amour*—as the Tailor's Dummy would put it—I'm immune to it. Why don't you direct your loaded questions to Arkady. You're not immune, are you?

ARINA. You're too smart for your own good. (*to TIMOFEICH who has entered:*) Clear the table, will you.

TIMOFEICH. Excuse me, sir. A patient here to see you —a woman.

VASSILY. Can't you see we're still eating, Timofeich? Tell her to come back tomorrow. (*to FEDKA who has entered wearing boots that are much too big for him:*) That's more like it. Good boy, Fedka.

BAZAROV. What's wrong with the woman?

TIMOFEICH. She's holding herself as if she was in pain. I think she has the gripes.

VASSILY. Dysentery—that's what she has. They call it the gripes about here. *Torminum,* Pliny calls it. Cicero uses the plural—*tormina.* (*to TIMOFEICH:*) Tell her to come back tomorrow morning.

BAZAROV. Let me have a look at her, Father.

VASSILY. No, no; you're on your holidays and—

BAZAROV. Please. I'd like to.

VASSILY. If you'd like to. Very well. Certainly. We'll only be a few—

BAZAROV. I'd prefer to see her by myself.

VASSILY. Off you go. Give her a good shot of opium —you'll find it in my bag on the desk in the study. She'll be most grateful—probably want to pray over you. (*BAZAROV has gone. VASSILY calls after him.*) And she'll offer you four eggs as payment. (*to ARKADY:*) Do you know how many eggs I was given last week? One hundred and seventy nine! That's no exaggeration, my pet, is it? (*TIMOFEICH is clearing the table. FEDKA helps him.*)

ARINA. (*sitting again*) Leave the table for the moment, Timofeich. Fedka, put those raspberries out in the pantry. (*Both servants leave.*)

ARINA. Are you an only child, too, Arkady?

ARKADY. Yes. No—no—I have a half-brother, Mitya.

ARINA. Is he at college?

ARKADY. He's eight months old.

VASSILY. He has a few weeks to wait yet. (*raising his glass*) Welcome again, Arkady. It's a great pleasure for us to have you here.

ARKADY. Thank you.

VASSILY. A very great pleasure. Isn't that correct, my pet?

ARINA. You're most welcome.

(*Now that they have ARKADY alone both parents want desperately to ply him with questions about their son. They move physically closer to him.*)

VASSILY. And I hope you can stay with us until you go back to college.

ARINA. You've forgotten, Vassily—Arkady has graduated.

VASSILY. Forgive me. Of course.

ARINA. And I'm sure he has hundreds of plans for the rest of the summer.

ARKADY. I haven't a plan in the world. I'm—at large!

VASSILY. Then you'll stay. Excellent. It's a delight for us to have Yevgeny's student friends. He usually brings somebody home with him every holiday. Fine young men all of them. And we love the company.

ARINA. Have you known Yevgeny long?

ARKADY. For about a year. We met at the philosophical meetings.

VASSILY. A philosopher, too, is he? Aha! That's a little detail we didn't know, did we?

ARINA. Has he got a girl in Petersburg?

ARKADY. Not that I know of.

VASSILY. I'm sure you have, Arkady; dozens of them.

ARINA. But nobody special?

ARKADY. Yevgeny? No; nobody special.

ARINA. He ate hardly any lunch. Is his appetite always as bad?

ARKADY. He's not very interested in food—maybe because I do the cooking!

ARINA. In this flat you share?

ARKADY. Yes.

ARINA. How many rooms do you have?

ARKADY. Three: bedroom, kitchen, washroom.

ARINA. And how long have you been together?

ARKADY. Oh, for the past year.

ARINA. What does he do about his laundry?

ARKADY. He does it himself. Mine, too. That's the arrangement.

VASSILY. Does he take any exercise?

ARKADY. He walks to lectures. And back. That's about it.

VASSILY. No good. He was always lazy about exercise. Not enough. Not nearly enough.

ARINA. How do you know when you don't know how far it is from the flat to the university? You just don't know. (*to ARKADY:*) And that hotel he mentioned — how many hours a week does he work there?

ARKADY. It varies. Sometimes twenty. Maybe up to thirty.

ARINA. And does he really make enough to feed and clothe himself?

ARKADY. Just about.

ARINA. And pay his fees?

ARKADY. We all live fairly frugally.

ARINA. You know he has never accepted any money from us, never since the first day he —

VASSILY. Arkady Nikolayevich is not interested in our domestic affairs, my pet. Tell me about this revolutionary stuff he was spouting last night, this — this — this —

ARKADY. Nihilism.

VASSILY. That's it. He's not really serious about that, is he? All that rubbish about —

ARKADY. We both are. Deadly serious.

VASSILY. Well, of course it is always valuable — and important, very important — most important to keep reassessing how we order our society. That's a very serious matter.

ARINA. I hope he wasn't serious when we were talking about that Madam Odintsov. He said I disliked her — that I hated her for some reason or other! That was very naughty of him.

ARKADY. He was only joking.

ARINA. I hope so.

ARKADY. You know he—

ARINA. (*rapidly*) Is he in love with her?

ARKADY. (*deeply confused*) With Anna? . . .
Yevgeny? . . . I—I—how would I know? How do you
tell? Maybe. I wouldn't know. I really wouldn't know.

VASSILY. And if he is, that's his own business, Arina.
There's just one question I'd like to ask you, Arkady—

ARINA. You've asked Arkady far too many questions.
Let him finish his tea.

VASSILY. With respect, my pet, it's you who have
asked the questions. My one question is this. In
Petersburg—in the university—in the circles you move
about in—how would he be assessed academically?
What I mean is, would he be considered run-of-the-mill,
average, perhaps below average—?

ARKADY. Yevgeny?! Below average?!

VASSILY. Yes?

ARKADY. Yevgeny is—well, he's the most brilliant
student in the university at present, probably one of the
most brilliant students ever there.

VASSILY. Yevgeny?

ARKADY. But you must know this yourselves. Yev-
geny Vassilyich is unique.

VASSILY. Unique?

ARKADY. Yes. Yes—yes—yes; absolutely unique.
And whatever he chooses to do, he's going to have a
dazzling future.

VASSILY. Are you listening, Arina?

ARKADY. Oh yes. You have an extra-ordinary son.

(*ARINA cries quietly. VASSILY cries quietly at first but
then his emotion gets the better of him. Unable to
contain himself, he grabs ARKADY's hand and
kisses it repeatedly.*)

VASSILY. Thank you. (*kiss*) Thank you — thank you — thank you. (*kiss*) You have made me the happiest man in Russia. (*kiss*) And now I'm going to make a confession: I idolize my son. So does his mother. We both do. Worship him. That's not incorrect, my pet, is it? And yet we daren't offer him even the most simple gesture of love, even of affection, because we know he detests any demonstration of emotion whatever. When you arrived here yesterday, I wanted to hold him, to hug him, to kiss him all over. But I daren't. I daren't. And I respect that attitude. It's my own attitude. What we must never forget is that we are talking here about an extra-ordinary man. And an extra-ordinary man cannot be judged by ordinary standards. An extra-ordinary man creates his own standards. Do you understand what I'm trying to say to you, Arkady?

ARKADY. Yes, I do.

VASSILY. A dazzling future — did you hear that, Arina?

ARINA. (*now recovered*) It's a beautiful day now.

VASSILY. There's no doubt in your mind?

ARKADY. None at all.

ARINA. We should all be out in the garden.

ARKADY. What area he'll move into I can't guess — science, philosophy, medicine, politics — he could be outstanding in any of them. But I do know he's going to be famous.

VASSILY. 'Going to be famous'. Non superbus sed humilis sum. Because some day, Arkady, some day when his biography is written, the following lines will appear: 'He was the son of a simple army doctor who from the beginning recognized his extra-ordinary talents and who despite every discouragement devoted his entire life and every penny he earned to his boy's education.'

(*BAZAROV Enters. He is instantly aware of the changed atmosphere and notices VASSILY putting away his handkerchief. ARINA gets quickly to her feet.*)

ARKADY. Ah, Dr Bazarov on call!

ARINA. It didn't take you long.

ARKADY. Where are the eggs? Did you not deserve a fee?

BAZAROV. The woman has a sprained wrist. All I had to do was strap it.

ARINA. Timofeich!

BAZAROV. What's been happening here?

ARINA. You boys are about to go out and get a bit of colour in your faces. (*to BAZAROV:*) Take Arkady round by the acacia plantation and down to the old mill.

VASSILY. I want to show them my herb garden first.

ARINA. I need you to help me put up new curtains in the study, Vassily.

BAZAROV. There's something going on here.

VASSILY. (*unable to contain his excitement any longer*) There certainly is something going on here. *Primo*: Arkady Nikolayevich has just decided to spend the rest of the summer here with us. *Secundo*: I have just decided to invite Anna and Katya Odintsov to come and have dinner here with us next Sunday.

ARINA. None of this has been—

VASSILY. Please. Allow me. And *tertio*: I have had a bottle of champagne in my study for the past three years —and now is the time to open it.

ARINA. We'll celebrate later, Vassily. We'll have your champagne at dinner tonight. Can you come into the study now?

VASSILY. Your curtains are much less important—

ARINA. Now. (*to BAZAROV and ARKADY:*) We'll

eat at seven. Have a nice walk. (*She catches VASSILY by the elbow and leads him quickly and firmly out.*)

BAZAROV. What's this all about?

ARKADY. What's what all about?

BAZAROV. You know damn well what I mean.

ARKADY. Just a moment, Bazarov. Just calm down. Your mother asked me what plans I had. I said none. Your father then said—excellent, spend the summer here.

BAZAROV. Fine—fine—fine. Spend the summer here. But you'll spend it here alone. And what's this about inviting Anna over here next Sunday?

ARKADY. You're shouting, Bazarov.

BAZAROV. How did that come up? Whose brilliant idea was that?

ARKADY. Your father's.

BAZAROV. Who else! The moment you used the words miniature empire I could see the peasant eyes dilate. Well, that is not going to happen! (*VASSILY puts his head around the door.*)

VASSILY. A patient outside. Sorry—am I intruding? Suffering from icterus. I have him on a diet of centaurion minus, carrots and St John's wort. Now I know you don't believe in medicine, Yevgeny, but I'd welcome your opinion on this. Not now, of course. Later. Later. Sorry. (*He withdraws.*)

BAZAROV. A whole summer of that? Icterus—do you hear him!—icterus! He couldn't say bloody jaundice, simple bloody jaundice like anybody else. And he's prescribing bloody cabbage water and bloody carrots! For jaundice! The man's a fool! That's what he is—a fool, a fool, a fool! And he's killing that poor bugger out there!

ARKADY. I like him.

BAZAROV. You like him.

ARKADY. He's a nice man.

BAZAROV. My mother's nice. My father's nice. The lunch was nice. Your Uncle Pavel is nice. I've no idea what the word means. Let's look at my father's life and see can we not find a more exact word. What does he do all day? Fusses about his garden. Dabbles in medicine. Bores my mother to death with his endless and pointless prattle. And he'll go on fussing and dabbling and boring until the whole insignificant little episode that was his trivial life is over. We can hardly call that nice, can we? What about futile?—fatuous?—would you risk ridiculous?

ARKADY. And your life is so meaningful, Bazarov, so significant?

BAZAROV. When we were out walking this morning we passed the new cottage that Father has just built for his bailiff and you said, 'Only when every peasant has a decent place like that to live in, only then will Russia be close to perfection. And it's our responsibility to bring that about.' And your face positively glowed with . . . niceness. And I thought to myself, I thought: there really is an unbridgeable chasm between Arkady and me. He thinks he loves those damned peasants. I know I hate them. But I know, too, that when the time comes I will risk everything, everything for them, and I'm not at all sure if Brother Arkady is prepared to risk anything. But of course the ironic thing is that those same damned peasants won't thank me—won't ever know of my existence. So there they'll be, all nice and cosy and smiling in their comfortable cottages and sending eggs up to Arkady in his big house; and Bazarov will be feeding the worms in some unmarked grave in the wilderness.

ARKADY. I don't know what your point is.

BAZAROV. That life is ridiculous and he doesn't know that it is.

ARKADY. And your life?

BAZAROV. Equally ridiculous. Maybe more ridiculous. But I'm aware that it is.

ARKADY. I'm going out for a walk.

BAZAROV. To be in good shape for the revolution or for Anna Sergeyevna?

ARKADY. If I stay we'll fight, Bazarov.

BAZAROV. Then by all means stay. Let's have a fight, Arkady. A fight between us is long overdue.

ARKADY. (*flushed with anger*) I'm fond of you, Bazarov. But there are times when I find your arrogance very hard to take. Only Bazarov has the capacity for real sacrifice. Only Bazarov is a fully authentic revolutionary. Only Bazarov has the courage and the clarity of purpose to live outside ordinary society, without attachments, beyond the consolation of the emotions.

BAZAROV. Yes, I have that courage. Have you?

ARKADY. I'm not as cleansed as you, Bazarov. I like being with people I'm fond of. I even love some people —if you know what that means.

BAZAROV. What what means?

ARKADY. Love—loving—do you know what loving means? (*pause*)

BAZAROV. Yes, I know what loving means, Arkady. I love my mother. I love her very much. And I love my father very much. I don't think there are two better people in the whole of Russia.

ARKADY. You don't behave like that.

BAZAROV. How do you expect me to behave? Kiss them? Hug them? Paw over them? You're talking like an idiot. Uncle Pavel would be proud of you.

ARKADY. What did you call Uncle Pavel?

BAZAROV. An idiot. The Tailor's Dummy is an idiot.

ARKADY. Bazarov, I'm warning you—

BAZAROV. It's interesting, you know, how deep-seated domestic attachments can be. Six weeks ago—a month ago you were preaching the dismantling of the whole apparatus of state, the social order, family life. But the moment I say your Uncle Pavel is an idiot, you revert to the old cultural stereotype. We're witnessing the death of a Nihilist and the birth—no, the rebirth of a very nice liberal gentleman.

(ARKADY goes rapidly and in sudden fury towards BAZAROV. He is almost certainly going to strike him when the door opens and VASSILY puts his head in. He speaks softly and is very embarrassed.)

VASSILY. There's something I—may I come in?— there's something I want to talk about to both of you. (*He comes in and closes the door behind him.*) You're sure I'm not intruding?

ARKADY. No, not at all.

VASSILY. Well. Before we eat this evening, a local priest, Father Alexei, is going to call on us. At your mother's request. She's a very devout woman, as you know, Yevgeny. Unlike myself, as you know, too. And the purpose of his visit is to—to—to gather the family around—your mother, myself in all probability, Yevgeny if he chooses, Arkady if he chooses—you'd be most welcome—to gather us all around in one large domestic circle—and—and—well, really to offer up some prayers of thanksgiving for your arrival home. A *Te Deum, Laudamus.* 'We praise Thee, Lord'. The little informal service will be held in my study—hence the new curtains. If you like to attend, please do. I can't tell you how grateful your mother would be if you did. But if you don't — and that's an attitude I'd respect, I certainly would — then — then — then don't. And we'll all meet for our celebratory dinner at seven. With champagne. And that's it. All right?

BAZAROV. Yes. I'll be at the service, Father.

VASSILY. (*delighted and relieved*) You will?!

BAZAROV. Why not. You and Mother would like me to be there.

VASSILY. Like you to?! We would —

BAZAROV. So I'll be there.

VASSILY. This is — this is just — just magnificent! Thank you, Yevgeny. Thank you from the bottom of my heart. You have no idea how much I appreciate that — how thrilled your mother will be!

BAZAROV. Not at all. (*to ARKADY:*) You'll join us, won't you? But if you'd prefer not to —

ARKADY. I'll join you of course. And sorry for losing my temper just now, Bazarov. I mean that. (*BAZAROV catches his hand.*)

BAZAROV. We were both a bit hasty. But I don't withdraw anything I said. (*ARINA Enters.*)

ARINA. Vassily, are you going to help me or are you not?

VASSILY. Arina! Good news! Great news!

BAZAROV. I'm just telling Father I'd be happy to attend the *Te Deum* service, Mother.

ARINA. Vassily?

VASSILY. Yes.

BAZAROV. It's this evening, isn't it?

VASSILY. Before we eat.

BAZAROV. Fine. As long as it's today some time. You see I'm leaving first thing in the morning.

ARINA. Leaving?

BAZAROV. Yes. I've exams in September and I've a lot of work to catch up with.

ARINA. But, son, you've only just arrived.

VASSILY. And you can study here, can't you? Amn't I right, my pet? My study is—

BAZAROV. My books are all at Arkady's home. I'll work there—if they will allow me. If they don't, I'll go back to Petersburg. But I'll come and see you for a night or two before next term begins. That's a solemn promise. Well. What time do you expect Father Alexei to arrive? When do we all sing the *Te Deum* together?

(*quick black*)

ACT TWO

Scene 1

*Late August. Just before noon. Scene as in Act One.
ANNA SERGEYEVNA and NIKOLAI have spent the
morning looking at accounts and touring the
Kirsanov estate. They have just returned. She is
alone on stage, sitting at a table, examining estate
maps and accounts with a quick and efficient eye.
BAZAROV enters. He is looking for ANNA but when
he sees her he pretends to be surprised. He is very
tense.*

BAZAROV. Ah. So you're back.

ANNA. Yes.

BAZAROV. The grand tour's over?

ANNA. Yes.

BAZAROV. It didn't take you long.

ANNA. A few hours.

BAZAROV. Nice day for it.

ANNA. Lovely.

BAZAROV. Beautiful. (*pause*) I think I left a book out
here somewhere . . . (*He looks around.*) Probably in
the living-room.

ANNA. (*just as he is about to Exit*) How are the studies
going?

BAZAROV. Well. No, not well.

ANNA. When do the exams begin?

BAZAROV. Early September. I didn't hear you come
back.

ANNA. Oh, we're back about half an hour.

BAZAROV. Really?

ANNA. Yes. Maybe an hour.

79

BAZAROV. I didn't hear you. Well, you couldn't have chosen a better day.

ANNA. Lovely.

BAZAROV. Beautiful. (*Pause. Then he moves beside her and speaks softly and with intensity.*) We've got to have a talk before you leave, Anna. Last Wednesday in your house you said something I've thought a lot about — (*He breaks off because NIKOLAI enters with another bundle of estate maps.*)

NIKOLAI. Leave a thing out of your hand for five minutes in this house and somebody's sure to lift it. D'you know where they were? In the pantry! Maps in the pantry! Bats in the belfry! Ha-ha! (*seeing BAZAROV*) Do you know where Arkady is, Yevgeny?

BAZAROV. Yes; he's gone for a swim with Katya.

NIKOLAI. I'm glad Master Arkady's enjoying himself. He ought to have been with Anna and me all morning. This is all going to be his one day and the sooner he masters the very complicated business of running an estate — (*He drops one of the maps. Picks it up quickly.*) — firmly and efficiently, the better. Now let's organize our lives. (*He sits at the table beside ANNA. BAZAROV goes off. ANNA watches him go.*) We had got the length of (*map*) number four. Where's five? — five? — five? — here we are. (*He spreads the fifth map across the table.*) Now. That's where we crossed the river. And somewhere about here — yes, there it is — that's the old well. Remember? — I pointed it out to you. (*aware that ANNA is not listening*) Are sure you're not exhausted?

ANNA. Not a bit.

NIKOLAI. Some tea? Coffee? Perhaps a glass of — ?

ANNA. I'm quite fresh. (*concentrating fully*) Let's carry on.

NIKOLAI. This is a tremendous help to me, Anna. I

can't tell you how grateful I am. Now. We drove along that road there and that's the area that is under wheat. The estate manager's cottage would be about here; Adam's house.

ANNA. And that's where the new threshing machine is sunk in the quagmire.

NIKOLAI. Yes.

ANNA. But that's clearly marked as a swamp ground.

NIKOLAI. Yes, it is, isn't it?

ANNA. Why didn't Adam take all the heavy machinery in from the far side?

NIKOLAI. I suppose he just — just took the short-cut.

ANNA. But he must have known he couldn't get across that swamp.

NIKOLAI. Do you think I should abandon it — the thresher?

ANNA. When your tenants have finished stripping it there won't be much of a thresher left.

NIKOLAI. That means I've lost the entire wheat crop.

ANNA. Where's the map of the land east of the river?

NIKOLAI. Here we are. These buildings are my new cheese and yogurt plant. I'm afraid I spent a great deal of money on those buildings. It hasn't been exactly an unqualified success, that plant.

ANNA. Did you sell any cheese at all last year?

NIKOLAI. Not a lot. Very little. None.

ANNA. Yogurt?

NIKOLAI. A few cases. But the cheese didn't go to loss. The poorer peasants were very grateful for it when —

ANNA. What map is that?

NIKOLAI. The stables — paddock — the area behind the house here —

ANNA. No, don't open it. I know that area. (*She checks some detail in an account book. He waits. Pause.*)

NIKOLAI. The Kirsanov estate; all five thousand acres of it. A bit of a mess, isn't it? What do you advise?

ANNA. Right. We're now in the last week of August. What I'll do is this. My crops are ready for harvesting. With a bit of organization I may be able to begin next Monday. That means that in two weeks' time all my machinery will be available. It will take—say—two days to transport it over here. So you must be ready to start the moment it arrives otherwise your wheat and corn and oats will have become too heavy and the thresher won't lift them.

NIKOLAI. But I can't possibly—

ANNA. I want to have another look at your cheese and yogurt accounts for the past year.

NIKOLAI. Of course, Piotr! Piotr!

ANNA. No, no; not now. Later. But from the quick look I had this morning it seems to me that the best thing you can do at this stage is cut your losses and close the dairy plant down.

NIKOLAI. My new plant? But it's only—

ANNA. I know you've spent a lot of money on the buildings but I think you can use them more profitably to store your wheat and oats and hay. You need more storage space anyway.

NIKOLAI. You're right.

ANNA. And finally you've got to sack that estate manager—what's his name?—Adam.

NIKOLAI. Sack my Adam?! Oh Anna, I'm afraid that's something I just couldn't—

ANNA. At best he's incompetent. And I suspect he may be corrupt. According to these records fifty foals were born last year and yet I counted only twelve yearlings this morning in the paddock.

NIKOLAI. There's an explanation for that. Apparently last winter wolves got into the enclosure and—

ANNA. That's his story. I've talked to Prokofyich. He says there have been no wolves around here for almost twenty years. You cannot run an estate this size unless you have a manager who is both competent and trutworthy.

(*PIOTR Enters, as usual breathless with haste and a bogus eagerness to serve.*)

PIOTR. You wanted me, sir?

NIKOLAI. Yes, Piotr?

PIOTR. You called me, sir.

NIKOLAI. I did?

PIOTR. No question about it, sir. I heard you myself.

NIKOLAI. I'm sure I did, Piotr. And I'm sure you pretended you didn't. (*to ANNA:*) Piotr's hearing is erratic.

PIOTR. That's unfair, sir. With the deepest respect, sir, that's a bit unfair.

NIKOLAI. I apologize, Piotr. Your hearing is perfect.

PIOTR. I was carrying logs into the kitchen, sir. The moment I heard you I dropped everything.

NIKOLAI. Very well, Piotr. I'm sure you did. Anyhow, I don't want you now. Here — take all this stuff with you. You know where to leave it.

PIOTR. I certainly do, sir. Leave it to Piotr, the man in the gap. (*He takes the maps and account books and exits.*)

NIKOLAI. The man in the gap! I don't know where he gets these expressions. Well. That's a splendid morning's work. Thank you again.

ANNA. I hope it's some help.

NIKOLAI. I really feel ashamed of — of — of my stewardship. I'm not trying to make excuses for myself but the whole place fell into my lap the year I graduated. I was the same age as Arkady is now. I knew nothing at all about the land . . . Anyhow. Invaluable. I do mean that. (*to BAZAROV who has entered as before:*) Ah, Yevgeny, taking a break from the books, eh? (*to ANNA:*) I keep telling him—he studies too much. Excellent. Spendid. I must tell Pavel about my plans. (*to BA-ZAROV:*) Anna Sergeyevna has clarified my thinking wonderfully. I'm going to close down the cheese and yogurt plant and I'm going to get rid of Adam, the estate manager. He is neither competent nor trustworthy. I'll be back shortly. (*He goes off. BAZAROF is as awkward and ill at ease as before. Pause.*)

ANNA. I don't think I clarified his thinking at all. (*pause*) He sounds full of purpose now but I wouldn't be surprised if some of the resolution is gone before he talks to Pavel. (*pause*) He thinks that his responsibilities ended when he gave the estate to the peasants to farm.

BAZAROV. I want to talk to you about a conversation you and I had last Wednesday at your house.

ANNA. Last Wednesday?

BAZAROV. It was just before dinner. We were sitting together in the conservatory. Somebody was playing a guitar in the distance. Katya's pup was lying between us and there was a circle of moisture where his nose rested on the tiled floor. You said I should offer him my handkerchief and I laughed very heartily because it sounded very, very funny . . . at that moment.

(*DUNYASHA appears briefly to do some housekeeping and exits immediately.*)

ANNA. For no reason at all that maid annoys me intensely.

BAZAROV. You were wearing a pale blue dress with a white collar and white lace cuffs. Anyhow Katya and

Arkady joined us at that point when I was just about to explain what I had meant a short time before when I had said that it seemed to me that we both appeared to act on the assumption that we talked to one another across some very wide chasm that seemed to separate us even though neither of us knew why that chasm was there, if indeed it was there; but because it seemed to both of us that it was, we behaved towards one another with a certain kind of formality that was more appropriate to people who had only just met . . . Probably none of this makes much sense to you. You probably don't remember any of it — do you?

ANNA. Yes, I do.

BAZAROV. Do you?

ANNA. Bits . . . fragments . . . more your intensity than what you said . . .

BAZAROV. It was a conversation of some importance to me and I'd just like to summarize it briefly — very briefly — if I may, and to say what I intended to say then if Katya and Arkady hadn't joined us and interrupted us . . . me . . .

ANNA. Katya and Arkady are having a long swim, aren't they?

BAZAROV. We were talking about relationships. We were talking about happiness. You said that for you happiness always seemed to be just that one step beyond your reach but that you still believed that some day you would grasp it. You said we had a lot in common; that you had been poor, too, and that you had been ambitious. You asked me what would become of me. I said I would probably end up a country doctor somewhere in the back of beyond and you said I didn't believe that for a minute but that I wasn't prepared to tell you what I really thought. You said you believed you could talk truthfully and openly about how you felt about things. I said I couldn't do that. You asked me why not. I said I always found it difficult to express exactly how I felt but that when I was with you I found it—found it even more difficult. And that's how the issue of a chasm between us came up. And how that chasm inhibited us—well, inhibited me. Because at the point when Katya and Arkady joined us, I was about to say that that chasm had prevented me from saying to you what I have wanted to say to you for weeks, what I have wanted to say to you ever since that very first day when we met here away back last May just after I had come from Petersburg—that I'm mad about you, Anna Sergeyevna, hopelessly, insanely, passionately, extravagantly, madly in love with you.

ANNA. Oh Yevgeny, Yevgeny—

BAZAROV. Yes, I am, I am. You know I am. I can't eat. I can't sleep. I can't study. I'm obsessed with you. I'm besotted by you. Let me kiss you, Anna. Please. Please let me kiss you. (*He takes her in his arms and kisses her. She does not free herself immediately. Then suddenly she pushes him away roughly.*)

ANNA. Yevgeny! Please! Oh, my God! You shouldn't have done that.

BAZAROV. Yes-yes-yes.

ANNA. No, you shouldn't. You've misunderstood the whole situation. You've misread the whole thing.

BAZAROV. No, I haven't, Anna. And you wanted me to kiss you. Admit that.

ANNA. Yes, you have, Yevgeny. Oh, yes, you have. Misread it totally. Oh, my God . . . (*She rushes into the house.*)

BAZAROV. Anna—! Anna, please—!

(*But she is gone. He is distraught. He does not know*

whether to run after her or to run away. Then he hears KATYA and ARKADY approach—they are laughing and calling to one another. He cannot escape that way. The only other hiding place is the gazebo. He rushes to it, sits down, pulls a book from his pocket, opens it at random and pretends to be immersed in it.)

ARKADY. (*off*) Give that shoe back to me!

KATYA. (*off*) I will not!

ARKADY. (*off*) Katya, I'm warning you.

KATYA. (*off*) Come and get it yourself. (*She runs on laughing; her hair wet, her towel flying, his shoe in her hand.*) O my God! (*She looks round frantically for somewhere to hide the shoe. She sees BAZAROV in the gazebo.*) I've got his shoe! He's going mad! Can I hide it here?

ARKADY. (*off*) Katya! Katya? (*She approaches BAZAROV and realizes at once that something is amiss. Pause.*)

KATYA. (*quietly, seriously*) Yevgeny? Are you all right, Yevgeny?

ARKADY. (*off*) Katya! Where are you? (*She gazes at him, hunched, tense, behind his book. She reaches out to touch him.*)

KATYA. Yevgeny?

ARKADY. You're for it, madam—I'm telling you! (*ARKADY is just outside. She withdraws her hand and runs out of the gazebo.*)

KATYA. I've hidden it in the gazebo, Arkady! (*She runs into the living-room and hides behind a door. ARKADY Enters, limping; a limp similar to his father's.*)

ARKADY. I'm warning you, girl! You've crippled me —that's what you've done! (*to himself:*) The gazebo . . . (*He goes to the gazebo and searches it. As he does:*) Was Katya here, Bazarov? Where did she hide my shoe? I'm going to kill that girl!

KATYA. (*appearing on the veranda*) Cold, Arkady. Very cold. Getting colder, much colder.

ARKADY. Come on, Katya! Where is it? Where is it? My feet are wrecked with bloody thorns!

KATYA. (*holding up a shoe*) This isn't yours, is it? (*She laughs and disappears into the living-room. He runs/hops after her. As he does:*)

ARKADY. You told me lies! You misled me! Just you wait there, madam! I'm going to twist your neck! Katya! Katya! Wait there! Wait!

(*He disappears into the living-room. Their laughter dies away. BAZAROV closes his book. He sits with his eyes shut tight, his shoulders tensed and hunched, his whole body rigid and anguished. FENICHKA enters carrying a large bunch of roses she has just cut. Just before she enters the house she glances over at the gazebo, thinks she sees somebody, looks again and recognizes BAZAROV. She approaches slowly and studies him for a few seconds before she speaks to him. She speaks softly.*)

FENICHKA. Yevgeny, is there something wrong? (*He opens his eyes suddenly. He is startled.*)

BAZAROV. Hello? — yes? — yes?

FENICHKA. Are you all right, Yevgeny? Is something the matter? (*He flashes a smile at her and speaks with excessive enthusiasm, almost in panic.*)

BAZAROV. Fenichka! It's you! How are you? I'm glad to see you — I'm delighted to see you! Yes, yes, I'm fine, I'm fine, I'm really fine, Fenichka. I mean that — I really

do — honestly. It's all over and I'm still alive. In fact I'm
perfectly well. But how are you? I haven't seen you for
days and days and I've missed you. Where have you been
hiding?

FENICHKA. You're the one who has been hiding —
upstairs reading those books of yours.

BAZAROV. Sit down beside me. Talk to me. (*She sits
beside him.*)

FENICHKA. What about?

BAZAROV. It doesn't matter. About chasms and rela-
tionships and happiness — about your healing presence
in this disturbed house — about those tranquil roses.
They're beautiful roses.

(*Sound of NIKOLAI playing the cello in the distance:
Beethoven's* Romance *for violin and orchestra in G-
major, op. 40.*)

FENICHKA. They're past their best. But Nikolai likes
to have flowers on the dining-room table.

BAZAROV. Nikolai is blessed. That's a strange word for
me to use — blessed. Six months ago I would have said
the word had no meaning. But it has — it describes the
condition of someone, anyone, to whom the beautiful
Fenichka turns her open face and on whom she smiles.
Yes, I have missed you. It's not that we ever talk — this is
probably the first time we've ever been alone together —
but I'm always aware of your presence in the house, even
when you're not there. I think it's because you generate
goodness. That's another strange word for me. And sud-
denly it has meaning, too. You're equipping me with a
new vocabulary, Fenichka!

FENICHKA. Will you stop talking like that, Yevgeny! I
don't understand a word you're saying!

BAZAROV. Are you happy, Fenichka? I hope you are. Are you?

(*He takes her hand in his. PAVEL Enters from the living-room. He is engrossed in a book. He pauses on the veranda and then moves slowly* D.S.)

FENICHKA. I don't think about things like that.

BAZAROV. Then you are.

FENICHKA. I'm young. I have my health. I have Mitya.

BAZAROV. And you have Nikolai. (*She withdraws her hand.*)

FENICHKA. Nikolai is a kind man.

BAZAROV. Yes, he is. Do you love him?

FENICHKA. Do you remember those drops you gave me for Mitya? Three days ago—remember?—he was vomiting—you thought he had eaten something. Well, they worked miracles. He was as right as rain in a couple of hours.

BAZAROV. I'm glad of that. So now you must pay me. (*FENICHKA is unsure and embarrassed.*)

FENICHKA. I—?

BAZAROV. Doctors have to be paid, don't they? Doctors are notoriously greedy people, aren't they?

FENICHKA. You're right, Yevgeny. I'm sorry. I'll speak to Nikolai today and he'll—

BAZAROV. No, no, no, no, no, no, Fenichka. I don't want money. It's not mere money I want. I want something personal—from you.

FENICHKA. What is that?

BAZAROV. Guess.

FENICHKA. I'm no good at guessing, Yevgeny.

BAZAROV. All right. I'll tell you what I want from you. I want . . . one of those roses. (*The cello music stops. She laughs with relief. He laughs with her.*)

FENICHKA. What colour would you like, sir?

BAZAROV. A red one. A small red one, Fenichka Fedosya.

FENICHKA. There you are, Yevgeny Vassilyich — one small red rose.

(*Between them they drop it. Together they stoop down to pick it up. Their hands meet on the ground. They laugh briefly and then stop. They look at one another. He kisses her on the lips. PAVEL is now D.S. and happens to look across at them at the moment they kiss. FENICHKA looks over BAZAROV's shoulder and sees PAVEL watching.*)

PAVEL. So this is how Nihilists betray hospitality.

FENICHKA. (*jumps to her feet and moves towards PAVEL*) There is nothing, Pavel Petrovich — I swear before God — there is nothing at all — (*she rushes off*)

BAZAROV. Fenichka, your flowers — (*He begins to pick them up.*)

PAVEL. What are your views on duelling, Monsieur Bazarov?

BAZAROV. Sorry?

PAVEL. I said what are your views on duelling?

BAZAROV. I have no 'views' on duelling.

PAVEL. Would you accept that it is a method by which gentlemen can settle their differences?

BAZAROV. I think it's just another method of killing — or being killed.

PAVEL. But if you were insulted you would demand satisfaction?

BAZAROV. I don't know. Maybe. I suppose so.

PAVEL. Excellent. (*BAZAROV has now gathered the scattered flowers and for the first time faces PAVEL.*)

BAZAROV. What's this all about?

PAVEL. I wish to fight you. (*BAZAROV now realizes that PAVEL is deadly serious.*)

BAZAROV. A duel? You want to fight a duel with me?!

PAVEL. Tomorrow morning at six.

BAZAROV. You're not serious!

PAVEL. Behind the birch plantation.

BAZAROV. But — but — but why would you want to fight with me?

PAVEL. It is sufficient for you to know that I despise you — indeed, I detest you.

BAZAROV. But that's no reason to *fight*, Pavel Petrovich! (*PAVEL raises his walking-stick as if to strike BAZAROV.*)

PAVEL. If you wish I'll give you a more immediate reason.

BAZAROV. You're serious! Good God, the man's serious!

PAVEL. We will use pistols at a distance of ten paces.

BAZAROV. I can't shoot.

PAVEL. Every gentleman can shoot.

BAZAROV. I haven't got a pistol.

PAVEL. We will use my pistols.

BAZAROV. I'm not taking part in this, Pavel.

PAVEL. We will dispense with seconds. I'll get Piotr to act as witness.

BAZAROV. Why are you doing this? What is this all — ?

PAVEL. Nobody else need be involved. Tomorrow morning at six, then.

BAZAROV. Good God Almighty! What in Christ's name is the — (*He stops suddenly because he suddenly knows the reason for the challenge.*) You're jealous, Pavel Petrovich! You saw me kisisng Fenichka and you thought —

PAVEL. Behind the birch plantation. Be there. (*He

moves away. NIKOLAI appears on the veranda. Neither PAVEL nor BAZAROV sees him nor hears him.)

NIKOLAI. Ah, Pavel. We should both go and have a word with—

BAZAROV. That's it! Of course! You're jealous, Pavel Petrovich! You're jealous because you're in love with Fenichka! O my God! (*remembering the duel*) O my God . . . (*NIKOLAI retreats into the living-room. BAZAROV drops into a seat.*)

SCENE 2

The following morning.
DUNYASHA is gathering up dishes that are on a table D.S.L. *close to the gazebo. She has only recently stopped crying—her face is red and she is snivelling. PROKOFYICH enters from the living-room. He is carrying a case which he leaves* U.S.L. *When DUNYASHA sees the case she sobs again.*

PROKOFYICH. Get a move on, Dunyasha. Don't spend all morning picking up a few dishes.

DUNYASHA. (*sotto voce*) Shut up, you old get.

PROKOFYICH. I'm talking to you, miss.

DUNYASHA. (*sotto voce*) Bugger off.

PROKOFYICH. The guest room is empty—at last. Change the sheets and the pillowcases and sweep the place out thoroughly.

DUNYASHA. Have I your permission to finish this job first, Prokofyich, sir?

PROKOFYICH. We'll do without your lip, missy. Then take the mattress and the floor mats and leave them out in the sun for the rest of the day. Maybe they should be fumigated. (*To PIOTR who has entered with another case:*) Come on, boy! Move! Move! Move! The sooner this house gets back to normal the better.

(*PROKOFYICH goes back into the house. PIOTR leaves his case beside the first and goes D.S. to join DUNYASHA. All the assurance, all the perkiness is gone. He is thoroughly wretched. He has to tell his story to somebody. DUNYASHA does not want to listen—she has her own grief. He holds out his hands. They are trembling.*)

PIOTR. Look, Dunyasha—look—look—I can't stop them—look. And my whole body feels as if it's trembling, too. Give me your hand—put it there (*his heart*)—it's galloping like a bloody horse; and about every ten minutes or so it stops—dead. (*She ignores him and continues working and snivelling.*)

DUNYASHA. Get out of my road, will you!

PIOTR. What—what—what's that?

DUNYASHA. You're in my way, Piotr!

PIOTR. (*almost in tears*) I don't hear a word you're saying, Dunyasha. As true as God's above. I'm as deaf as a post.

DUNYASHA. So you've told me.

PIOTR. What happened was this—

DUNYASHA. I don't want to hear about it.

PIOTR. Yevgeny was about there and I was about here and the Tailor's Dummy was about there—(*trembling hand*)—look!—didn't I tell you—there!—there!—there! God, the sight of this is going to break my mammy's heart. Anyway, Yevgeny and the Tailor's Dummy had their backs to one another; and just when they were about to turn to face each other, Yevgeny called me to him and he whispered, 'How do you cock a gun, Piotr?' and the sweat's standing out on his forehead and he's holding the gun like this and his eyes are half-shut and he's facing the other way. 'How do you cock a gun?'—for Christ's sake! And I'm standing as close to him as I am to you now and I reach over to pull the hammer back and he sort of turns towards me and whatever messing we're both at, suddenly, suddenly there's this huge explosion right beside my cheek —

PROKOFYICH. (*on the veranda*) Piotr!

PIOTR. —and I thought, my God, I thought, he's blown my head off—

DUNYASHA. You're wanted, Piotr.

PIOTR. —because I fell to the ground and I could hear nothing and see nothing and feel nothing. And then the smoke cleared and there, lying across a fallen birch tree, there's—(*PROKOFYICH has come up behind PIOTR and now grips him by the arm.*)

PROKOFYICH. Are you a guest here, boy?

PIOTR. What's that, Prokofyich? I think my drums are ruptured.

PROKOFYICH. (*very loudly into his face*) Can you hear me now, Piotr?

PIOTR. Shouting's no help, Prokofyich.

PROKOFYICH. If you don't get back to work at once — at once!—I'll rupture your head, Piotr. Harness the carriage. Bring it round to the back. Now! (*He pushes PIOTR roughly. PIOTR goes off L. PROKOFYICH now turns to DUNYASHA. She is wiping the surface of the table.*) That's all right. Leave it now. No need to make a meal of it. Get upstairs and clean out that guest-room. (*As he is about to go off L.:*)

DUNYASHA. I'm thinking of leaving, Prokofyich.

PROKOFYICH. (*without hesitating*) Don't think about it, miss. Just leave.

DUNYASHA. Well, if I do, I won't do it just because you would want me to do it. If I do it, I'll do it because I want to . . . (*But he has already gone. She wipes her nose, lifts her tray and goes towards the house. Just as she approaches the veranda steps, ARKADY and PAVEL and NIKOLAI come out of the living-room. PAVEL is very pale and his arm is in a sling. ARKADY comes first, walking backwards. NIKOLAI holds PAVEL's 'good' arm even though PAVEL has a walking-stick. ARKADY and NIKOLAI fuss over him as if he were very ill. He is barely able to keep his temper.*)

ARKADY. Careful, Uncle Pavel, careful.

NIKOLAI. Watch that step.

ARKADY. Take it slowly. There's no rush.

NIKOLAI. (*to DUNYASHA:*) Watch, girl. Out of the way.

ARKADY. Get a cushion, Dunyasha. Two cushions. (*She goes into the house.*)

NIKOLAI. Let me take that stick, Pavel, and you can hold on to my arm.

ARKADY. (*preparing a seat*) Here we are, Uncle Pavel.

NIKOLAI. Turn it round. He doesn't like the direct sun. Splendid. Now get something for his feet.

PAVEL. (*groans*) O my God . . .

NIKOLAI. (*misunderstanding the groan*) I know you're in pain. Hang on for another second. That's it now, Pavel—here we are. Sink back into that—gently—gently—that's it—lovely. Can you lean forward a little? (*He slips a cushion behind PAVEL.*) Excellent. (*At the same time ARKADY puts the second cushion, which DUNYASHA has brought, on a stool and slips the stool under PAVEL's feet.*) Thank you, Arkady. Now we're more comfortable, aren't we? (*DUNYASHA leaves.*)

ARKADY. Should I get a lower stool?

NIKOLAI. I think that's about right. (*to PAVEL:*) That bandage isn't too tight, is it?

ARKADY. He lost a lot of blood, you know.

NIKOLAI. As long as the fingers are free to —

PAVEL. (*almost a shout*) Please! (*now softly and controlled*) S'il vous plaît. I got a superficial cut. I lost a few drops of blood. I am properly bandaged. I am in no pain.

NIKOLAI. Pavel, you have been through a shocking —

PAVEL. I am perfectly well and perfectly comfortable, thank you very much, and I would be very grateful if both of you would leave me alone now. There's a green-backed book sitting on the couch in the conservatory, Arkady. Would you bring it to me? (*ARKADY goes into the house. Pause.*) I owe you an apology, Nikolai. I am sorry to have caused all this . . . upset. I apologize. I won't mention it again. (*Pause. PAVEL puts perfume on his hands.*) If anybody's going into town today, I'd be grateful if they'd get me some eau-de-Cologne. (*pause*) I overheard young Katya talking to her sister yesterday afternoon. She referred to me as 'beau-de-Cologne'. Not bad, I thought. I like that little lady. Spirited. (*pause*) And I understand Bazarov is leaving us.

NIKOLAI. Why did you have the duel with him, Pavel?

PAVEL. It was my fault entirely.

NIKOLAI. What did you fight about?

PAVEL. We had a political disagreement.

NIKOLAI. What about?

PAVEL. I don't wish to discuss it further, Nikolai.

NIKOLAI. I would like you to tell me exactly what the disagreement was about, Pavel. (*ARKADY returns with the book.*)

ARKADY. *The Castles of Athlin and Dunbayne* — is this it?

PAVEL. Set in Scotland. The Wonderful Mrs Ann

Ward Radcliffe. She's charming—she understands nothing.

ARKADY. There's something I'd like to say, Uncle Pavel. Formally. In my father's presence.

PAVEL. Oh dear—a manifesto.

ARKADY. Because I brought Bazarov to this house, I feel at least partly responsible for whatever happened this morning—I know now I shouldn't have brought him here in the first place but—

NIKOLAI. Nonsense, Arkady. This is your home.

ARKADY. I'm trying to be rational and fair, Father. Our friendship was very important to me. It still is. So I want to be fair to that friendship and at the same time I don't want to judge anybody quickly or rashly. So I'm afraid I must ask you, Uncle Pavel, to tell me exactly, if you would, please, exactly what—

PAVEL. Exactly—exactly—exactly! Why this sudden passion for exactitude? Very well. Let's get the damned thing said once and for all. But first I want a promise from you both that what I am going to tell you will not be repeated by either of you to anybody. Do I have that assurance? (*They both nod.*)

ARKADY. Of course you do.

PAVEL. Well. Monsieur Bazarov and I were talking about English politicians. About Sir Robert Peel, to be exact, and his family background. I said Peel's father was a wealthy land-owner. Bazarov said he was a cotton manufacturer. I've looked it up since. I was wrong. Bazarov was in the right. Not that that matters—the issue itself was trivial. But one word, as they say, borrowed another. Tempers, as they say, too, flared. In a moment of irrationality I challenged him to a duel. He was astonished—naturally. And he met me this morning merely to flatter my pathetic pride. All in all he behaved admirably. His gun went off accidentally. I fired into the air. I have acquired some respect for Monsieur Bazarov. Some modest respect. (*pause*) I will never mention that episode ever again. (*pause*) Now will somebody please tell me why Prokofyich is stumping about the house like an enraged beast?

ARKADY. He disliked Bazarov from the beginning. Now he believes he has a reason to hate him.

PAVEL. Isn't he a loyal soul? Life must be very simple for him. (*PIOTR enters from the left, exactly as we saw him at the beginning of the scene.*)

PIOTR. The carriage is waiting in the yard, sir. (*Immediately after he makes his announcement PIOTR turns and goes off L.*)

NIKOLAI. Thank you, Piotr. Oh, Piotr — my straw hat's in the hall. Would you bring it to — Piotr! Piotr! My God, did you see that! He ignored me! The insolent pup ignored me! Oh-ho, Master Piotr is certainly going to go. There are going to be changes about here. I'm not going to be insulted in my own house by a servant or by anybody else.

PAVEL. I don't think he heard you, Nikolai.

NIKOLAI. (*violently*) That's a damned lie! And you know that's a damned lie! The bastard never hears me! Never! Never! I'm sick of him never hearing me! Sick to death of it! (*quickly recovering*) Forgive me . . . I'm sorry . . . That was unpardonable . . . Forgive me . . . I think I'll play the cello for a while . . . The cello, I find, is very . . . healing . . . (*He goes into the house. ARKADY is astonished at the outburst. PAVEL has some idea why it happened.*)

PAVEL. Good Lord. What was that all about?

ARKADY. He never really warmed to Bazarov either.

PAVEL. Perhaps.

ARKADY. I know Bazarov likes him very much but he can't show affection easily.

PAVEL. What are his plans?

ARKADY. He intended going to Petersburg to study. But when he was packing this morning he got a message that there's a typhus epidemic in his home province; so he's going there first to help his father out.

PAVEL. Ah. Very worthy. I'm thinking of moving out myself.

ARKADY. What do you mean?

PAVEL. Just going away. Leaving.

ARKADY. Where to?

PAVEL. Germany, France. England. Maybe Scotland! Perhaps I should buy the castle of Dunbayne?

ARKADY. You don't mean leaving for good, Uncle Pavel, do you?!

PAVEL. We'll see. But certainly not until after the harvest is saved. They couldn't save the hay without my muscle, could they? Ah, Monsieur Bazarov. I hear you're going home?

(*BAZAROV Enters* L. *with a book in his hand. He is dressed for travelling. He leaves his jacket beside his cases and comes down to ARKADY and PAVEL. This is now a fully mature young man — neither in his clothes nor in his demeanour is there any trace of the student. His manner is brisk, efficient, almost icy.*)

BAZAROV. How is the arm?

PAVEL. Fine, thank you. You dressed it well.

BAZAROV. Take the bandage off after three days and let the fresh air at the wound.

(*The sound of NIKOLAI playing the cello:* Romance *in F-Major, Op. 50.*)

PAVEL. Le malade n'est pas à plaindre qui a la guérison en sa manche.
BAZAROV. I don't speak French.
PAVEL. Montaigne. It means: don't pity the sick man who — (*BAZAROV turns abruptly away from him.*)
BAZAROV. (*to ARKADY.*) I must say goodbye to your father.

(*He goes towards his cases. ARKADY follows him, takes his arm and speaks to him quietly, privately, in an attempt to restore the old intimacy. PAVEL goes off to the far side of the garden and reads.*)

ARKADY. I have a plan, Bazarov. I'll go to Petersburg at Christmas; back to the old flat; and we'll —
BAZAROV. No, you won't do that, Arkady. By Christmas you and Katya will probably be married. (*They continue this conservation as BAZAROV opens a case and puts his book into it.*)
ARKADY. Married?! Me?! For God's sake, a man, we Nihilists don't believe in —
BAZAROV. And I'm pleased for you. She'll take you in hand and you want to be taken in hand. You're naturally complementary. And natural elements that complement one another tend to create a balanced and stable unit.
ARKADY. Cut that out, Bazarov! Stop addressing me, man! This is your old matie, Arkady, your old cook and bottle washer. And what I'm going to do is fix a date for a big reunion. Immediately after you finish your exams!

— mid-September! I'll go to Petersburg. We'll get a keg of beer. We'll get all the boys from the old cell together and —

BAZAROV. We won't be getting together again, Arkady. We both know that. We are saying goodbye now. From your point of view you're making all the sensible choices because instinctively you know you're not equipped for our harsh and bitter and lonely life.

ARKADY. Who the hell do you mean by 'our', Bazarov? I'm a Nihilist, too, remember?

BAZAROV. When you were a student. But your heart never really forsook the gentry and the public decencies and the acceptable decorum. Of course you have courage and of course you have your honest passion. But it's a gentleman's courage and a gentleman's passion. You are concerned about 'difficult issues' but you believe they are settled by rational, gentlemanly debate and if that doesn't work, by gentlemanly duels. But that's not how real change, radical change is brought about, Arkady. The world won't be remade by discussion and mock battles at dawn. As you told your uncle a long, long time ago we're long past the stage of social analysis. We are now into the era of hostilities — of scratching, hurting, biting, mauling, cutting, bruising, spitting. You're not equipped for those indecencies. When it would come to the bit you would retreat into well-bred indignation and well-bred resignation. Your upbringing has provided you with that let-out. Mine didn't. I am committed to the last, mean, savage, glorious, shaming extreme.

ARKADY. I see.

BAZAROV. To be blunt with you, Arkady: you are not good enough for us.

ARKADY. Was it that savage, shaming side of you that frightened Anna Sergeyevna off? I shouldn't have said that. Forgive me, Bazarov. (*BAZAROV responds as calmly and as coldly as before.*)

BAZAROV. No need to apologize. I may very well have frightened Anna Sergeyevna. But if that is what happened, I have no regrets. Miniature empires have no appeal to me. My sights are trained on a much, much larger territory. We had a good year together, Arkady. Thank you for that.

ARKADY. Bazarov, I still think we should — (*He stops because FENICHKA has come from the living-room and joins them. She has a package of sandwiches for BAZAROV.*)

FENICHKA. So you're all set.

BAZAROV. Yes.

FENICHKA. Did someone say something about a typhus epidemic?

BAZAROV. My father. He likes dramatic language. It's all probably a ruse to get me home.

FENICHKA. Well, don't take any unnecessary risks, Doctor. I made a few sandwiches for the journey. I know you like cold lamb.

BAZAROV. Thank you very much. (*The conversation is punctuated by the awkward silences that farewells create.*)

ARKADY. Who's driving you?

BAZAROV. Prokofyich. He volunteered.

FENICHKA. You're honoured. He doesn't drive me.

BAZAROV. He's just making sure he's getting rid of me. (*Brief laughter. Silence.*) I must say goodbye to your father.

ARKADY. Yes.

FENICHKA. He told me he prefers playing piano duets with Katya to playing the cello by himself.

ARKADY. Yes, I think he enjoys the duets.

FENICHKA. He says Katya is as good as your mother.

ARKADY. Did he say that? (*DUNYASHA appears at the living-room door.*)

DUNYASHA. (*calls*) Fenichka.

FENICHKA. Yes? (*DUNYASHA beckons.*) What is it? (*FENICHKA goes to DUNYASHA.*)

ARKADY. Dunyasha's suddenly very coy. (*DUNYASHA gives the bottle of milk to FENICHKA. They exchange a few words. DUNYASHA keeps her face averted.*)

BAZAROV. (*calls*) Goodbye, Dunyasha. (*DUNYASHA disappears. FENICHKA returns.*)

FENICHKA. She has a very bad head-cold. This is a bottle of milk for the journey. She says to say goodbye.

BAZAROV. Thank her for me, will you?

FENICHKA. I will.

BAZAROV. I think she thought I wasn't sticking at the books enough: she kept bringing cups of tea up to my room. (*silence*)

ARKADY. He's talking about going away, too. Uncle Pavel. France. Germany. Scotland, maybe!

FENICHKA. For a holiday?

ARKADY. For good, he says.

BAZAROV. You'll have an empty house.

FENICHKA. He's not serious, is he?

ARKADY. I think he is.

FENICHKA. When is he leaving?

ARKADY. After the harvest is in. He wants to do his share of the scything.

FENICHKA. Pavel?!

ARKADY. Yes!

FENICHKA. You're joking!

ARKADY. No, I'm not. Yes, of course I am.

FENICHKA. Pavel scything! Can you imagine?

Shh . . . (*Again the brief laughter. The cello stops. Silence. PAVEL moves towards them.*)

PAVEL. Are the beautiful Katya and Anna joining us for dinner tonight?

ARKADY. Great! (*recovering*) Are they? That's news to me.

PAVEL. Am I wrong?

FENICHKA. It's tomorrow night.

ARKADY. I thought it was Sunday

PAVEL. (*looking straight at FENICHKA*) Ah. Then I was wrong. Yet again.

FENICHKA. They're coming straight here after church. That was the arrangement.

PAVEL. (*still looking straight at FENICHKA*) My mistake. I get things wrong, Fenichka. Sorry.

FENICHKA. Tomorrow night.

PAVEL. I see. *Bon. Bon.*

BAZAROV. I think I should call Prokofyich.

ARKADY. (*holding on*) Katya has finally chosen a name for her pup, Pavel.

PAVEL. Pup? What pup?

ARKADY. The borzoi pup she got from us at the beginning of the summer! She's going to call it Pavel! (*Brief laughter. NIKOLAI joins them.*)

PAVEL. I suppose it's one way to be remembered?

NIKOLAI. We're all ready for departure, are we, Yevgeny? Good. Great. And Piotr's driving you, is he? Good. Excellent. (*calls*) Piotr!

ARKADY. Prokofyich's taking him, Father.

NIKOLAI. Prokofyich? (*softly*) Much better. Much more reliable. You should be in Petersburg well before night.

BAZAROV. I'm not going to Petersburg. I'm going home.

NIKOLAI. Good. Good. Excellent in fact. I'm sure your parents will be delighted to have you. Indeed. Just as we were.

BAZAROV. Thank you for all your hospitality, Nikolai Petrovich.

NIKOLAI. It was my pleasure. It was our pleasure. We'll all miss you — won't we? I'll miss all those early morning walks we had — occasionally. And Pavel will miss those — those — those stirring political discussions. And Arkady will miss the student banter. And Fenichka — Fenichka — Fenichka will miss your excellent medical advice — won't you? And — (*PROKOFYICH appears* L. *Absurdly stiff-backed and formal. He stares at a point above everybody's head.*)

PROKOFYICH. (*loudly*) I beg your pardon.

NIKOLAI. What is it, Prokofyich?

PROKOFYICH. The carriage is about to depart.

NIKOLAI. Yes, we know, Prokofyich. Thank you.

PROKOFYICH. I merely mention the fact in case any person wishes to travel in it. (*He lifts the cases and exits stiffly. They stare after him in astonishment and amusement. A quick, stifled giggle from FENICHKA. One from ARKADY. Then FENICHKA explodes. Then they all laugh, excessively, in relief. BAZAROV only smiles. He observes the happy family group from the outside.*)

NIKOLAI. Shhh! He'll hear you.

ARKADY. He couldn't — he couldn't even look at us!

NIKOLAI. I know — I know —

ARKADY. In case any person — any person wishes to travel in it!

FENICHKA. It's going to be a-a-a- (*She breaks down again.*)

PAVEL. A what?

FENICHKA. Can't say it.

Nikolai. Shhh!

Arkady. I know what she's trying to — (*breaks down*)

Pavel. A what?

Fenichka. It's going to be a very chatty journey! (*Again they explode. Then as suddenly the laughter dies. Silence.*)

Nikolai. Oh dear — oh dear — oh dear.

Arkady. It was that eye fixed on the sky.

Fenichka. I know. And the shoulders back.

Nikolai. Poor old Prokofyich. But we mean no harm, do we? No, no; we mean no harm at all.

Arkady. About to depart. Oh, I'm sore. Very sore. (*Silence. BAZAROV goes to NIKOLAI.*)

Bazarov. Again, thank you for everything.

Nikolai. You'll come and stay with us again — perhaps. (*They shake hands. BAZAROV now goes to PAVEL.*)

Bazarov. (*bows*) Pavel Petrovich. (*They shake hands.*)

Pavel. Thank you. *Adieu.* (*BAZAROV goes to FENICHKA. He takes her hand.*)

Bazarov. I wish you every happiness, Fenichka. Take care of yourself.

Fenichka. You, too, Yevgeny. (*He goes to ARKADY and hold out his hand.*)

Bazarov. Arkady. (*ARKADY hesitates and then impulsively embraces him.*)

Arkady. I don't give a damn what you say! Mid-September! After the exams! That's settled. And make it two kegs. (*He releases BAZAROV. He is crying.*) Come, you twisted, perverse bastard! Clear out to hell! Move! Move! (*He pushes BAZAROV in front of him. They exit. NIKOLAI follows them, then PAVEL.*) He's coming, Prokofyich! Here's your passenger! (*FENICHKA is alone on stage. She listens to the voices off. The lines overlap.*)

NIKOLAI. (*off*) Put the bags at your feet.

ARKADY. (*off*) Where's your jacket?

PAVEL. (*off*) Good luck, Yevgeny.

BAZAROV. (*off*) Thank you very much.

ARKADY. (*off*) All set?

BAZAROV. (*off*) I left a book somewhere.

ARKADY. (*off*) It's in your hand. Fool.

BAZAROV. (*off*) Thank you again.

NIKOLAI. (*off*) Good luck with the exams.

ARKADY. (*off*) Mid-September. That's settled.

PAVEL. (*off*) Have a good journey.

ARKADY. (*off*) Give my love to your father and mother.

BAZAROV. (*off*) Goodbye.

ARKADY. (*off*) Write me, Bazarov.

BAZAROV. (*off*) I will.

NIKOLAI. (*off*) Goodbye.

PAVEL. (*off*) Goodbye.

(*A chorus of goodbyes. FENICHKA waves tentatively and says 'goodbye' quietly. DUNYASHA, who has been watching from the living-room, now comes down and stands behind FENICHKA. FENICHKA turns and sees her. She is sobbing helplessly.*)

DUNYASHA. All he had to do, Fenichka — all he had to do was raise his little finger and I'd have kissed his feet.

FENICHKA. Oh, Dunyasha —

DUNYASHA. Oh God, I would have, Fenichka. Just raise his little finger. (*She throws her arms around FENICHKA and sobs. FENICHKA holds her.*)

FENICHKA. Shhh. I know, Dunyasha. I know. I know.

SCENE 3

*Early September. Afternoon. The dining-room in the
Bazarov home. VASSILY is standing at the head of
the table, always on the point of lighting his pipe.
ARKADY is sitting at the bottom of the table, immo-
bile, staring at the ground. (This is not where he sat in
Act One Scene 3.) He is scarcely aware that VAS-
SILY is speaking. VASSILY is smiling as fixedly as
in Act One and is even more breezy and energetic.
But the energy is spurious and it is soon apparent
that occasionally he forgets what he is saying —
hence the repetitions in his speech — and that he is on
the point of breakdown.*

VASSILY. Yes, yes, that was a memorable lunch. I
recall every detail of that lunch with total clarity. Oh yes,
that was one of the happiest occasions ever in this house.
We'd been expecting you for so long, you see — for years,
for heaven's sake! And now here you were, in this very
room, around this very table. And all I can say now —
and I was aware of it then, too — was that your presence
alone quickened these ancient bones again. *Omnia ani-
mat, format, alit,* as Cicero says . . . *omnia ani-
mat* . . . That doesn't sound like Cicero, does
it? . . . Oh yes, that was a lunch to remember. That's
the event that furnished us with the richest and warmest
memories — that's not inaccurate, my pet, is it? . . .
(*He looks around. Realizes she is not there.*) Where had
she placed us? I was here. And she was there. And you
were sitting where you're sitting now. And Yevgeny was
over there. And I have one particularly vivid recollec-
tion. I had just told you that story of the retired major
who practises medicine 'just for the good of the commu-

nity'; and the two of you gazed at me for a second and then suddenly collapsed with laughter; and there you both are, spread across the table, convulsed, unable to speak! Oh, that's a particularly vivid memory. 'Just for the good of the community.' Couldn't move. Couldn't speak. (*TIMOFEICH shuffles in. He seems even more decrepit than before. He begins pottering aimlessly with the dishes on the table.*) And Timofeich was looking after us as usual, weren't you, Timofeich?

TIMOFEICH. She's awake.

(*VASSILY, suddenly alert, leads TIMOFEICH to the side so that ARKADY will not hear the conversation. ARKADY is scarcely aware that TIMOFEICH is there.*)

VASSILY. Well?

TIMOFEICH. No change.

VASSILY. Did she speak?

TIMOFEICH. Not a word.

VASSILY. Is she still in bed?

TIMOFEICH. She's in the study.

VASSILY. What's she doing there?

TIMOFEICH. Sitting.

VASSILY. On the couch?

TIMOFEICH. On the swivel chair. You should comb her hair for her. (*TIMOFEICH returns to the table.*)

VASSILY. Leave that stuff, Timofeich. And stay with her, will you?

TIMOFEICH. She can't go on without food in her. You should get her to eat.

VASSILY. (*sudden fear*) Where's my medicine bag, Timofeich? (*TIMOFEICH points to a high shelf where the bag is almost hidden.*) Ah! Good man. Thank you. Thank you.

TIMOFEICH. What are you thanking me for? You hid it there yourself. (*TIMOFEICH exits. VASSILY assumes the smile again and the breezy manner.*)

VASSILY. He's been a tower of strength to me, old Timofeich. I don't know what I'd have done without him.

ARKADY. How is Arina Vlassyevna?

VASSILY. She'll be with us in a while. Arina Vlassyevna is — what's the cliché? — she is as comfortable as can be expected — everything considered — considering everything. But we were discussing that lunch, weren't we? Oh, that was a memorable occasion. Do you happen to remember a boy who helped at table that day? — a very young boy? — in his bare feet? — Fedka? I have a confession to make about Fedka: Fedka wasn't a servant of ours at all. We hired Fedka for that occasion. To impress you, my friend. To give Yevgeny's background that tiny bit of extra weight. *Vanitas vanitatum et omnia vanitas.* Ecclesiastes, I think. But don't trust me on that. I can still quote with some accuracy but the attribution . . . the attribution seems to . . . That lunch, yes. And Fedka. I had asked Father Alexei could he recommend somebody. And what did he present us with? — the butcher's second son with the running nose and not a shoe to his name — in a manner of speaking. Serving at the table, barefoot! Good Lord. I can laugh at it now. I remember I said, 'Arkady Nikolayevich will think he's staying with some sort of primitives.' And Yevgeny lifted his head — you know how he lifts his face and turns it slightly sideways — and gave me that sharp, quick eye of his — and he said — he said — and nobody's wittier than Yevgeny as you well know — he lifted his head and he gave me — gave me — (*He breaks down: Sudden, uncontrollable sobbing. He recovers almost immediately.*) I should pray to God, they say. How can I go on?—that's what I say to God. How do you expect me to go on?—I say. What do you think we're made of?—I say. (*pause*)

ARKADY. It was very late when I got back from Petersburg. My father was waiting up for me. 'I've got very bad news for you, son. I can't tell you how bad the news is.' 'It's Bazarov,' I said. 'Yes,' he said. 'It's Bazarov.' (*pause*)

VASSILY. At the end of that first week there were so many people sick and dying that we decided to split up: he took the whole town and the region to the north and west. I had the south and east. Some nights he didn't get home at all. And when the epidemic spread to the neighbouring province we didn't see him for days on end. 'All for the bloody peasants,' he said to me. 'Everything for the bloody peasants, damn them!' And then I came in this night—it was Friday—amn't I correct, my pet? There was a light under his bedroom door. And I was tiptoeing past when he called me. He was sitting up in the bed, propped up against the pillow; and even though the candle was behind his head the first thing I noticed was how bright, how bright his eyes shone. And he said in that ironic tone of his, 'Father,' he said, 'I'm going to make you a present of a much larger practice. I'm going to present you with the town and the region to the north and west.' 'What does that mean?' I said. (*His voice begins to waver.*) 'It means,' he said—'It means,' he said—'It means that I'm considering retiring. What's your opinion of this, Dr Bazarov? Does it look like typhus?' And he pulled up the sleeve of his night-shirt and held his bare arm over to the candle and there were the purple blotches. (*ARKADY is now crying quietly.*)

ARKADY. I'm sorry for behaving like this . . .

VASSILY. There was nothing we could do. His mother made him lime-flower tea and she tried to feed him spoonfuls of beetroot and cabbage soup. But he was too weak to swallow anything. And the next morning — that was Sunday — amn't I right, my pet? — yes, I am — that was Sunday — he opened his eyes and said, 'Do something for me, Father. Send a messenger to Anna Sergeyevna Odintsov and tell her that Yevgeny Vassilyich Bazarov is dying.'

ARKADY. All Katya knew was that a messenger came to the house and that within five minutes Anna was gone.

VASSILY. And late that same evening a grey carriage with red wheels and drawn by four horses drew up at our door and a footman in dark green livery opened the carriage door and this lady in a black veil and a black mantle got out. She told me she was Anna Sergeyevna Odintsov and asked to see my son. I argued with her. I said it was too dangerous. But she was determined. So I brought her to him. I left them together. She stayed with him for half an hour. He was too weak to talk. She just sat with him and held his hand.

ARKADY. Nobody has seen her since. She didn't go home when she left here. She sent the carriage home and she went on to Moscow. She probably wants to be by herself for a while.

VASSILY. He passed away that same evening. His mother sent for Father Alexei. He was dead by then but Father Alexei gave him the last rites anyway.

ARKADY. My father didn't know what to do. I was somewhere in the Petersburg area buying a new thresher — that's all he knew. But where I was staying — how to get in touch with me — he was at his wits' end. Finally he sent Piotr to look for me — just to walk the streets of Petersburg and look for me. And all the time I was in our old flat. That never occurred to them.

VASSILY. We tried to get word to some friends. Timofeich did the best he could. I thought it best to have a short wake because of the nature of the illness and because his mother was a little . . . *perturbata*. So we buried him on Monday morning, early. A quiet funeral; his mother, Father Alexei, Timofeich, myself. And Fedka, the worthy Fedka, properly shod. It was nice of him to come. And brave. A few prayers. Flowers. The usual. I'll take you there if you wish. It's only a ten-minute walk. But if you prefer not . . . some people find cemeteries . . . difficult. There's something not right about a father burying his son, isn't there? Some disorder in the proper ordering of things, isn't it? It's not the way things should be, is it?

ARKADY. He was the best friend I ever had, Vassily Ivanyich. (*pause*)

VASSILY. (*almost in a whisper but with a sudden and astonishing passion*) Damn you, Almighty Father! I will not stand for it! I certainly will not stand for it!

ARKADY. He was the only real friend I ever had.

VASSILY. What's that?

ARKADY. (*suddenly resolute*) I'm going to carry on his work, Vassily Ivanyich! I'm going to dedicate myself to his memory and to the work he was so involved in! I have none of his brains and none of his talent. But whatever talent I have and whatever energy I have I will give to the revolution, to Bazarov's revolution.

VASSILY. (*dreamily*) Oh, yes. Politics are very important.

ARKADY. He never thought I was capable of much. But I am! I am! And I am now more than ever because I'm doing it for him! (*VASSILY pats him on the shoulder.*)

VASSILY. Every so often he would regain consciousness. One time he opened his eyes and he said, 'I am no loss to Russia. A cobbler would be a loss to Russia. A butcher would be a loss. A tailor would be a loss. I am no loss.' It never occurred to him the loss he'd be to his mother and me.

ARKADY. If you would take me to the cemetery, I'd like to make my solemn promise to him there.

(*ARINA enters, her hair dishevelled, wearing slippers and an odd assortment of clothes. When she enters her face is vacant. Then she sees VASSILY and she smiles. VASSILY greets her with great warmth and enthusiasm. ARKADY gets to his feet.*)

VASSILY. Ah — Arina! Now that's an improvement! Now you're looking really well, my pet! Do you know that you slept for almost three hours? And who's going to do the housework if my wife lies in bed and spends the day sleeping? Tell me that, my sweet and beautiful wife? And look who's here! Look who's come to see us! (*She looks blankly at ARKADY.*) Yes! It's Arkady, my pet! It is, indeed! Arkady Nikolayevich! The very moment he heard he came straight over. He was afraid he'd have to leave without seeing you.

ARKADY. All I can say, Arina Vlasseyevna — (*He begins to cry again.*) — all I can say is that — that — that — that I'm shattered, just shattered.

VASSILY. We've looked after ourselves as you can see. But what we've got to do now is get you something to eat. What can I offer you? What would tempt you? I have it! Arina Vlassyevna is partial to a cup of blackcurrant tea! The very thing!

ARKADY. I'll never forgive myself that I wasn't here. I was away in Petersburg. I didn't hear a thing until late last night.

VASSILY. (*breezy, busy*) One small cup of blackcur-

rant tea and two very tiny but very appetizing home-
made biscuits—that's what this aristocratic lady re-
quires and that is what she is going to eat. What does
Cicero say? *Tantum cibi et potionis*—we should drink
and eat just enough to restore our strength—no more,
no less.

ARKADY. I can't tell you how devastated I am. I know
I'll never get over it.

(*ARINA now sits. Pause. She looks at ARKADY as if she
were trying to remember him, as if she were going to
speak to him. Her face is placid, child-like, almost
smiling. And when she sings it is the gentle, high-
pitched voice of a very young girl.*)

ARINA. (*sings*) *Te Deum laudamus: te Dominum con-
fitemur. Te aeternum Patrem omnis terra veneratur.*

(*As soon as she begins singing ARKADY looks in alarm
at VASSILY. VASSILY responds by putting his
finger to his lips and shaking his head as if to say—
Say nothing; don't interrupt. Then he sits beside his
wife, puts both arms round her, and sings with her
and directly to her:*)

VASSILY/ARINA. *Tibi omnes Angeli, tibi Caeli et uni-
versae Potestates. Tibi Cherubim et Seraphim incessa-
bili voce proclament:*
Sanctus, Sanctus, Sanctus, Dominus Deus Sabaoth.

(*Slowly bring down the lights as they sing together.*)

Scene 4

*After dinner. Early October . The lawn-garden in front of
the Kirsanov home.
ARKADY is standing at the piano and singing 'Drink to
me only'. He sight-reads the words. KATYA accom-
panies him. ANNA sits by herself in the living-room,
listening to the music.
PAVEL stands on the veranda.*

   Pavel. (*sings very softly*)
'But might I of Jove's nectar sup,
I would not change for thine.'
   Fenichka. Very nice, Pavel.

(*PAVEL realizing that he has been overheard wags his
finger in admonition. He then lapses into his own
private thoughts. Two or three times we hear the faint
sound of dance music played on the piano-accordion
some distance away. These brief coincidences of the
two sounds — the piano and the piano-accordion —
produce an almost eerie noise. The PRINCESS is
sitting alone D.S.R., partly concealed behind her un-
necessary parasol, vigorously masticating and every
so often brushing her sleeve and skirt. PROKO-
FYICH and PIOTR have assembled a large trestle-
table in the centre of the lawn. They now cover it with
a white cloth and arrange chairs around it. FEN-
ICHKA oversees this work with a proprietorial eye.
She is now very much mistress of the house and fully
at ease in PAVEL's presence. PIOTR, slightly intox-
icated, is completely restored to health and cockiness
and jaunty self-assurance. He nips down behind the*

*gazebo on the pretext of getting a chair and tosses
back a quick, secret drink from a hip-flask. He is
about to pour a second drink when the PRINCESS
calls him.)*

PRINCESS. You, boy! Come here! Come here! Come
here! (*He quickly hides his flask and does a little dance as
he goes to her.)*

PIOTR. Princess, can I help you?

PRINCESS. What's that noise?

PIOTR. That noise, Princess, is Arkady singing and
Miss Katya playing the piano for —

PRINCESS. The noise! The damn noise! There — d'you
hear that?

PIOTR. My apologies. That is the musician getting
ready for tonight — the annual harvest dance. We hold it
in the granary.

PRINCESS. Musician? What musician?

PIOTR. A piano-accordion player, Princess. He comes
from the town of Orel.

PRINCESS. My brother, Josef, had the first accordion
ever brought into Russia. My father lit a bonfire in the
yard and burned the damn thing before the whole house-
hold. Then he whipped Josef with his own hunting crop
until he apologized publicly to everybody — family and
servants. Ha-ha. That ended damn accordions in our
house!

PIOTR. I'm sure it did.

PRINCESS. Josef was black and blue for a month. Tell
your friend from Orel that story. Ha-ha. Whipped him!
Whipped him! Whipped him!

PIOTR. I'll tell him, Princess. (*She withdraws. PIOTR
returns to his work. PAVEL comes down and joins
FENICHKA.)*

PAVEL. I bought that song-book in London — oh, it must be twenty-five years ago. (*suddenly remembering*) I know exactly when I bought it — the day they made Arthur Wellesley foreign secretary. We were out on the town, celebrating!

FENICHKA. Who was that, Pavel?

PAVEL. Arthur? The first Duke of Wellington. Good man. Good fun. We had a lot of laughs together . . . Nice time of the day, this.

FENICHKA. Lovely.

PAVEL. Nice time of the year. Do you like October, Olga?

PRINCESS. I detest every month — for different reasons.

PAVEL. It's my favourite season, the autumn. I tell myself it's the one time of the year when the environment and my nature are perfectly attuned.

PRINCESS. It seems to me you tell yourself a lot of rubbish. And you'd need to be careful — the way you carry yourself — you could be mistaken for an accordion player.

PAVEL. I beg your pardon?

PRINCESS. You look very like one to me, with your shoulders so far back.

PAVEL. (*to FENICHKA:*) I didn't catch what she said. I could be a — ?

FENICHKA. An accordion player.

PAVEL. Me?!

PRINCESS. They all carry their shoulders back. That's because the weight is all down the front here. Ha-ha, you could end up being whipped by mistake!

PAVEL. Good heavens, could I? (*to FENICHKA:*) Why do they whip accordion players?

FENICHKA. I don't know. Do they?

PAVEL. So it seems.

FENICHKA. (*to PIOTR:*) There's a vase of dahlias and a vase of chrysanthemums outside the pantry door. Put the dahlias here and the chrysanthemums there.

PIOTR. Anything the lady wishes.

PAVEL. Arkady has a pleasing voice. From the mother's side of the house. Maria had a sweet voice.

FENICHKA. (*to PIOTR as he dances off:*) And napkins from the linen-press. On the top shelf. (*to PAVEL:*) What is that song?

PAVEL. 'Drink to me only'.

FENICHKA. I never heard him singing that before.

PAVEL. (*speaks*)
'I sent thee late a rosy wreath,
Not so much honouring thee
As giving it a hope that there
It could not withered be . . .'

(*FENICHKA has been counting the chairs.*)

FENICHKA. Sorry, Pavel—what was that?

PAVEL. Nothing. Just mumbling to myself. (*DUNYA-SHA Enters* L.)

FENICHKA. I've noticed you doing that a lot recently. You're not beginning to dote, are you? There are only wine glasses here, Dunyasha. Bring out the champagne glasses, will you?

(*PAVEL, wounded, moves away. DUNYASHA is so excited she can scarcely keep her voice down. FENICHKA continues moving around the table, adjusting the settings. DUNYASHA follows her. FENICHKA listens with interest but her manner hints that the days of confidences are over.*)

DUNYASHA. Brilliant news, Fenichka! Absolutely brilliant! The aunt died at half past three this morning! Can you believe it!

FENICHKA. Who?

DUNYASHA. The aunt—the old aunt—the old bitch that reared Adam!

FENICHKA. Oh, I'm sorry to hear—

DUNYASHA. He'll be able to sell her cottage. And she has left him about two hundred roubles. And he wants to get married, Fenichka!

FENICHKA. To you?

DUNYASHA. Jesus, you don't think he fancies the Tailor's Dummy, do you?!

FENICHKA. Dunyasha, I—

DUNYASHA. Of course it's to me! At five this morning —the old cow couldn't have been right stiff—he was up banging on my bedroom door: 'Little one, will you make me the happiest man in Russia?' That's what he said! Can a duck swim, says I to myself. He didn't go back to the corp-house till well after nine. Jesus, you should have seen that glossy black 'tash of his twitching! D'you know what we should do, Fenichka?—you hang on for another couple of months and we'll get married together! Wouldn't that be a howl! A double wedding! Drive the poor old Tailor's Dummy astray in the head altogether!

FENICHKA. I don't want you to call Pavel Petrovich by that name again, Dunyasha.

DUNYASHA. The Tailor's Dummy? Between ourselves, for God's sake; it's only to you and Piotr and—

FENICHKA. I never want to hear it again.

DUNYASHA. Are you—?

FENICHKA. Is that clearly understood? Good. I'm sorry about the old aunt. But Adam should have no regrets: he was more than attentive to her. I'll take those napkins from you, Piotr; thank you. You arranged those flowers beautifully, Dunyasha. I'm glad you're thinking of marrying him. He'll make a very reliable husband. Now—what's missing? The champagne glasses. (*to DUNYASHA:*) Would you get them for me? (*DUNYASHA stumps off.*) No, the other way round, Piotr—the dahlias on this side. Don't you think so?

PIOTR. I'm sure you're right. The dahlias are left-handed. (*While he was out PIOTR has had a few more drinks.*) What else can I do for you, Fenichka? You just tell Piotr.

FENICHKA. That's all for now.

PIOTR. Have you enough chairs?

FENICHKA. I think so.

PIOTR. What about some stools?

FENICHKA. They won't be needed.

PIOTR. Stools are a very efficient means of seating large numbers of guests in an outdoor environment, Fenichka.

FENICHKA. We haven't got large numbers, Piotr.

PIOTR. Once again you are right. Another few bottles of wine, perhaps?

FENICHKA. (*dismissing him*) Thank you, Piotr.

PIOTR. I know a poem. Would you like me to recite it?

FENICHKA. Not now, Piotr.

PIOTR. Later perhaps. I could spell chrysanthemum for you.

FENICHKA. That is all for the time being, Piotr.

PIOTR. Well, as soon as the time being is up, Piotr will be at your elbow and at your command. (*He bows formally and goes off L.*)

FENICHKA. The harvest party has begun early. (*She holds up an empty bottle.*) Since lunch time. (*To ANNA who comes out:*) Come and join us, Anna.

ANNA. The days are shortening already, aren't they? (*She pauses beside the PRINCESS.*) Are you all right, Auntie?

PRINCESS. Why do you always ask that absurd question when you know the answer. No, I am not all right. There's a constant buzzing in my head. I can scarcely walk with arthritis. That meal they gave us was inedible. And I am about to be sick with the smell of cat in this damn place. (*She rises and leaves* L.) When you're ready to leave you'll find me in the paddock. There's a black filly there that needs to be broken.

ANNA. She gets great comfort from her misery.

PAVEL. I'm studying her carefully. We could have a lot in common.

FENICHKA. You don't have her vigour, Pavel.

PAVEL. I could simulate that, too, couldn't I?

FENICHKA. Nikolai tells me you had a good harvest.

ANNA. I was away for most of it. Yes, it was a good harvest. (*She gestures her indifference.*) The best I've ever had . . . It's good to hear Arkady singing.

FENICHKA. Yes.

ANNA. And Katerina tells me he's out and about again.

FENICHKA. He hadn't much choice. The estate's his now. He was needed on the land.

ANNA. They're a handsome couple.

PAVEL. Aren't they.

ANNA. A pity you'll miss the wedding, Pavel.

FENICHKA. The weddings, Anna.

ANNA. Of course.

PAVEL. Yes, I'm sorry about that. I'm due to arrive in Zurich that day. (*FENICHKA waters the plants in front of the veranda.*) Any news of the epidemic? — the typhus epidemic?

ANNA. I'm told it's almost died out.

PAVEL. Has it?

ANNA. So I've heard.

PAVEL. Ah. Good.

ANNA. Yes.

PAVEL. So it's over now?

ANNA. Almost. Not quite.

PAVEL. Good. They cause great devastation, those things. But they pass — they pass.

ANNA. That's true.

PAVEL. And the world carries on.

ANNA. I suppose so. Yes, of course it does. (*pause*)

PAVEL. I got to know him slightly just before he left here. I hadn't understood him at all before that. In my stupidity. He was a fine man.

ANNA. He was also a . . . difficult man.

PAVEL. He was that, too.

ANNA. He wanted to marry me.

PAVEL. I gathered that.

ANNA. (*crying quietly*) I should have married him, Pavel . . .

PAVEL. Perhaps — perhaps.

ANNA. Oh, yes, I should. Oh, yes. It would have been a difficult marriage but I should have married him. It's very hard to carry on when you know you've made so enormous a mistake, Pavel. How do you carry on?

PAVEL. I wish I could help you, Anna. I very much wish I could help you. I have no answers to anything. We all want to believe at least in the possibility of one great love. And when we cannot achieve it — because it isn't achievable — we waste our lives pursuing surrogates; at least those of us who are very foolish do.

FENICHKA. Soon be time to bring them inside.

PAVEL. And that's no life, no life at all. (*He puts his*

hands on ANNA's shoulders.) A kind of contentment is available, Anna: in routine, acceptance, duty.

ANNA. I had that life.

PAVEL. It has its consolations. Is that a terrible thing to say?

ANNA. He thought so.

PAVEL. I know. But it's the only threadbare wisdom I have for you. I don't believe a word of it myself.

(*DUNYASHA enters with the glasses. She barely conceals her fury.*)

DUNYASHA. Miss, the champagne glasses, miss.

FENICHKA. (*very calm*) Thank you, Dunyasha. Put them on the table.

DUNYASHA. Is there anything else I can get you, miss?

FENICHKA. That will be all for now, Dunyasha.

DUNYASHA. Sir, what about you, sir?

PAVEL. Sorry?

DUNYASHA. Sir, can I get you anything, sir?

PAVEL. (*alarmed at this attention*) Me? No, nothing . . . nothing, thank you.

(*DUNYASHA stumps off into the house. NIKOLAI enters from the L. He is wearing a very brightly coloured jacket — a jacket for a much younger man. Now and again bring up the sound of distant piano-accordion music.*)

NIKOLAI. I've held you all up, have I?

FENICHKA. I thought you'd gone dancing by yourself.

NIKOLAI. Ha-ha. Just saying a word of formal thanks and encouragement to the workers for their sterling efforts over the past weeks. (*quick kiss and embrace for*

FENICHKA) This looks splendid! Excellent! I love those dahlias.

FENICHKA. These are the dahlias.

NIKOLAI. Are they? I never get them right. They're beautiful anyhow. (*to all:*) Incidentally some time later on it would be greatly appreciated if we all put in a brief appearance at the dance; just to—you know—just to —to pass ourselves. No obligation whatever to—to participate—not that some of us could—(*indicates his lameness*)—even if we wished to. I'll ask Arkady to dance with you on my behalf—just once!

PAVEL. You'll have to let me have one dance, too, Nikolai.

NIKOLAI. Yes?

PAVEL. Of course. The brother-in-law to be. I was an excellent dancer once upon a time. (*to FENICHKA:*) That's agreed, then.

NIKOLAI. Good. Good. Yes. Fine. Anyhow. Now to organize our lives. Is everybody here? (*He looks into the living-room where KATYA and ARKADY are talking heatedly.*) Look at those two love-birds. (*KATYA bangs the piano-lid shut.*)

FENICHKA. Squabbling love-birds.

NIKOLAI. Arkady! Katya! Come out here at once! Where's the Princess?

ANNA. She's walking around somewhere.

NIKOLAI. I'll go and get her.

ANNA. No. Leave her. She's happier by herself. (*KATYA and ARKADY join the others.*)

ARKADY. Well—well—well—well! (*ironic clapping*) Feast your eyes on that wonderful sight!

NIKOLAI. What's the matter?

ARKADY. Just look at that astonishing jacket! Where did that come from?

NIKOLAI. I agree with you, Arkady. I think myself it's much too young for a man of—

FENICHKA. I chose it, Arkady.

ARKADY. Did you now?

FENICHKA. And I think he's very handsome in it.

KATYA. So he is. And it's a wonderful jacket. (*to ARKADY:*) We all agree.

ARKADY. I'm sure you do. I still think it's remarkable. (*NIKOLAI does a mock pirouette.*)

NIKOLAI. What do you think, Anna?

ANNA. (*in a reverie*) Sorry—sorry?

NIKOLAI. Do you approve of it?

ANNA. Approve of—?

PAVEL. (*quickly*) We all think you're gorgeous, Nikolai. And I'm madly jealous. One Tailor's Dummy in the house is sufficient.

NIKOLAI. Who is the Tailor's Dummy?

PAVEL. Didn't you know? That's what the servants call me.

NIKOLAI. I never heard that, Pavel.

PAVEL. I don't mind in the least. It's not without affection, is it?

FENICHKA. Show them the lining, Nikolai.

NIKOLAI. I certainly will not!

FENICHKA. Go on! For my sake. (*With mock coyness NIKOLAI unbuttons the jacket and opens it to reveal an even more brilliant lining. Applause and laughter.*)

NIKOLAI. And this, of course, is the real Nikolai Petrovich.

FENICHKA. Feast your eyes on that!

KATYA. Yes—yes—yes—yes!

ARKADY. Ridiculous.

FENICHKA. And when he's tired of it, I'm going to wear it—inside out.

NIKOLAI. Enough of this. I'm not sure you're all taking a hand at me. Let's all gather round the table and get a glass. There's going to be no formality. And no speeches. Just an exchange of congratulations and good wishes between friends. Come over here beside me, Fenichka. Has everybody got something in his glass?

KATYA. (*filling her glass*) Just a second, Nikolai.

NIKOLAI. Give me your hand, Katya. Good. Splendid. Well. The harvest is saved. It has been a good, an especially good, year. And first of all we want to thank you most warmly, Anna—don't we, Arkady?—most warmly indeed for all the tremendous help you have been to us not only in your advice and wisdom over the past months but more particularly, indeed most particularly, for your spontaneous and generous offer of your machinery—an offer, may I say—

ARKADY. You said no speeches.

NIKOLAI. And there'll be none.

ARKADY. Good. Thank you, Anna.

NIKOLAI. Thank you most sincerely, Anna. And if the situation is ever—

ARKADY. Father!

NIKOLAI. Sorry—sorry. Thank you. We all thank Anna—don't we? (*Clapping. Raising of glasses.*)

FENICHKA. Incidentally did you hear that Adam's old aunt has died?

NIKOLAI. Somebody did mention that. When did it happen?

FENICHKA. Early this morning. Are you still thinking of sacking him?

NIKOLAI. Yes. No. He worked like a Trojan this past month. But this is a matter for you, Arkady. You're master of the estate now.

ARKADY. I'll think about it. I'll watch him. He knows he's on probation.

NIKOLAI. Why do you ask?

FENICHKA. No reason. Just wondering. Who's for more wine?

KATYA. Me, please. We're all going to miss you very much, Uncle Pavel.

PAVEL. For all of two minutes.

ARKADY. I think you've had enough wine, Katya.

KATYA, (*dismissively*) I'll make that decision. (*to PAVEL:*) Yes, we will. A whole lot.

PAVEL. (*to KATYA:*) Did I hear you playing 'Drink to me only'?

KATYA. And Arkady was singing. Weren't you? (*ARKADY ignores her.*)

NIKOLAI. That used to be my song . . . long ago . . . Shakespeare wrote the words — did you know that?

PAVEL. No.

NIKOLAI. Yes, he did.

PAVEL. Jonson.

NIKOLAI. What's that, Pavel?

PAVEL. A contemporary of Shakespeare.

NIKOLAI. Yes?

PAVEL. Ben Jonson.

NIKOLAI. What about him?

PAVEL. He wrote the words.

NIKOLAI. What words?

PAVEL. Ben Jonson.

NIKOLAI. Who is this Ben Jonson, Pavel?

PAVEL. Nothing — nothing — just that you said that Shakespeare wrote the words of —

PAVEL. (*shouts*) Who cares! (*controlled*) Who cares who wrote the bloody words! Who gives a damn! Exactly four weeks ago today Bazarov died — and who cares about that? — Who even remembers? Not even one of you! All you care about is stupid jackets and big harvests and stupid bloody songs! Well, I care. And I remember. And I will always remember. And in the coming years I'm going to devote my life to his beliefs and his philosophy—to our philosophy—to carrying out his revolution. That's what I'm going to do for the rest of my life. And nothing in the world—absolutely nothing—is going to stop me!

(*He breaks down and cries. There is a long, embarrassed silence. KATYA pours another drink. NIKOLAI, unable to endure the silence, begins to hum but tails off quickly. Silence again. Then FENICHKA goes to NIKOLAI and whispers in his ear.*)

NIKOLAI. Sorry? What's that?
FENICHKA. The books.
NIKOLAI. Books? What books? Oh the books! Of course! Piotr'll get them for me. P—(*He is about to shout 'Piotr!'—and miraculously there is PIOTR, now very drunk, at his elbow.*) Ah. There you are, Piotr. Isn't that remarkable?
PIOTR. Sir.
NIKOLAI. I didn't call you, did I?
PIOTR. Yes, sir, you did.
NIKOLAI. Did I?
PIOTR. With great clarity. Twice. And here I am.
NIKOLAI. Well, if you say so, Piotr. Splendid. Run up to my bedroom and on the table beside my bed you'll find two books. Bring them here to me, will you? (*pause*)
PIOTR. C-h-r-y-s-
NIKOLAI. Sorry? What's that?
PIOTR. C-h-r-y-s-a-n-t-
NIKOLAI. What's he saying?
PIOTR. -r-y-s-a-n-t-m-t-m-r-s-y-

(The others laugh. PROKOFYICH, stiff and stern, Enters.)

NIKOLAI. You're not intoxicated, Piotr, are you?
PIOTR. I know it. I'm telling you I know it. Let me try again. C-h-r-s-y-

(PROKOFYICH leads PIOTR off L.)

PROKOFYICH. Come on, boy. You're for bed. *(to all:)* Sorry about this. It won't happen again. Come on. Move, boy. *(to all:)* You know you are all cordially invited to the dance later on.
NIKOLAI. Thank you, Prokofyich. We'll go for a short time.
PROKOFYICH. Very good. I'm sorry about this. *(They exit; PIOTR still trying to spell.)*
KATYA. I'll get those books, Nikolai.
NIKOLAI. Poor old Piotr. Poor boy must be suffering terribly.
FENICHKA. He's been at it since lunch-time.
PAVEL. And it's time I went and got some packing done. I hope the wedding—no, weddings—will be a great success. I'm sure they will. *(produces a tiny box)* I have ordered a proper present—it's due to arrive at the end of the week. In the meantime—it's only a token. *(He hands the box to FENICHKA.)*
FENICHKA. Thank you very much, Pavel.
NIKOLAI. What is this?
FENICHKA. It's a ring. It's beautiful, Pavel, really beautiful. Thank you.
NIKOLAI. Let me see. *(FENICHKA kisses PAVEL on the cheek.)*
PAVEL. Make it two dances.

NIKOLAI. Lovely, Pavel. Thank you very much. What's engraved on the stone? Is it a sphinz?

PAVEL. Is it? It's only a token. No value whatever.

FENICHKA. I don't believe that.

NIKOLAI. Put it on.

FENICHKA. I love it. I'll think of you every time I wear it.

NIKOLAI. It's a beautiful memento, Pavel.

PAVEL. *Magnifique*! That's two occasions I'll be recalled: whenever you wear that ring; and every time borzoi fanciers get together and Katya's damned pup is discussed. (*to ARKADY:*) I've ordered something for you and Katya, too. I hope you'll like it.

ARKADY. Thank you — from both of us. (*KATYA returns with two books.*)

KATYA. Here you are.

NIKOLAI. Thank you, Katya. And these are for you, Pavel. Something to read on your journeyings.

PAVEL. What's this?

NIKOLAI. Fenichka chose them. We hope you like them.

PAVEL. Mrs Ann Ward Radcliffe! Never! *The Romance of the Forest* and *The Mysteries of Udolpho.* Wonderful! Where did you get them? They've been out of print for years!

FENICHKA. Piotr hunted them out when he was in Petersburg last month.

PAVEL. Absolutely wonderful! You couldn't have given me greater pleasure! Darling, innocent Mrs Ann Ward Radcliffe. And the two I'm missing. Can I bear so much intellectual stimulation? (*General laughter. He kisses FENICHKA and then NIKOLAI.*)

FENICHKA. Brother — brother Pavel.

PAVEL. I'll carry them with me wherever I go. *Merci. Merci beaucoup.*

NIKOLAI. (*wiping away his tears*) Now. One final toast. Yes, I'm sorry, Arkady. I'm going to make a short speech—a very short speech.

KATYA. I would like to hear a very long speech.

NIKOLAI. What I just want to say is that this house, this home, is about to suffer a permanent and irreparable loss. Pavel is leaving. We will miss him terribly. And I want him to know that wherever he goes, our love will accompany him always, everywhere. But there is a silver lining to—to—to every—We do have a compensation, indeed a very substantial compensation. Fenichka Fedosya has consented to be my wife and for that—that—that benediction I am profoundly grateful. And on the same day—this day two weeks, amn't I correct?—and on this very lawn another marriage will be celebrated between Katya Sergeyevna and my son, Arkady. And by that union, too, I am profoundly gratified. Some people might think that there is something inappropriate about a father and a son getting married on the same day, some disorder in the proper ordering of things. But I know that for both of us it will be an occasion of great joy and great fulfilment. And who is to determine what is the proper ordering of things? (*Bring up the accordion playing 'Drink to me only'.*)

FENICHKA. Listen, Nikolai.

NIKOLAI. (*to KATYA:*) That clever musician—he picked it up from you. (*They all listen for a few seconds.*) That was our song, long, long ago. Maria and I. I sang the melody and she sang the seconds. Our party piece. Her eyelids fluttered when she sang. Shakespeare wrote the words—did you know that? (*He begins to sing. FENICHKA watches him with a strained smile. He puts his arm around her and hugs her.*) Sing! (*She gives him an uncertain smile but does not sing. KATYA moves beside ARKADY. She catches his hand. She begins to sing and*

sings the words directly into his face. He does not sing.
PAVEL moves across to ANNA who is sitting away from
the others. He catches her hand.)

PAVEL. Do you sing?

ANNA. Occasionally. When I'm alone.

PAVEL. Yes. *Je comprends* . . .

NIKOLAI/KATYA.

Drink to me only with thine eyes,
And I will pledge with mine;
Or leave a kiss but in the cup
And I'll not look for wine.
The thirst that from the soul doth rise
Doth ask a drink divine;
But might I of Jove's nectar sup,
I would not change for thine.

COSTUME PLOT

Arkady

Scene 1
Grey wool coat
Brown breeches
Tan stripe shirt
Cap
Brown boots
Belt
Socks

Scene 2
Same boots, belt, breeches
Ivory peasant shirt
Gray tweed vest

Scene 3
Same as I-1
Wool coat on set

Bazarov

Scene 1
Black/brown wool coat
Grey breeches
Black & ivory striped shirt
Cap
Black boots
Belt
Socks

Scene 2
Same breeches, boots, belt
Blue & ivory striped shirt

Scene 3
Same as I-1

Nickolai

Scene 1
Rust hacking jacket w/matching vest
Corduroy breeches
Ivory cotton shirt
Black/wine patterned stock
Socks
Brown boots

Scene 2
Black tail suit
Ivory silk vest
Formal dickie
Blacks socks
Black ankle boots
Ivory silk stock
Blue paisley scarf

Pavel

Scene 1
Wine frock coat
Blue patterned vest
Ivory silk dickie
Breeches
Grey jacquard stock
Black ankle boots
Black socks
Wig (personal)
Mustache (LWT)

Scene 2
Black tail suit
Ivory silk vest
Ivory silk dickie w/lace

Ivory Jacquard stock
Patent formal pumps
Same socks, wig, mustache

Vassily

Scene 3
Black frock coat
Striped vest
Striped shirt
Black pants
Black socks
Black ankle boots
Cotton scarf

Prokofyich

Scene 1
Brown carriage coat
Ivory shirt
Rust tweed breeches
Black boots
Socks
Sash
Hat
Tan vest

Scene 2
Same shirt, vest, boots, breeches, sash
Rose livery coat (Burbank)

Arkady

Scene 1
Tan stripe pants
Tan strip shirt
Suede boots (carry on)

Scene 2
Brown tweed breeches
Ivory jacquard shirt
Grey jacquard vest
Black ankle boots
Black socks
Brown patterned stock

Scene 3
Same as 2-2
Add brown frock coat
Scene 4
Take off coat top of scene
Same as 2-1
Add coat end of scene

Bazarov

Scene 1
Grey breeches
Ivory shirt
Vest
Black boots
Socks

Scene 2
Same as 2-1
Add coat & cap

Nickolai

Scene 1
Same as 1-1
Change to rust pattern vest
Straw hat

Scene 2
Same as 2-1
Change to black ankle boots
Black breeches

Scene 4
Same as 2-2
Change to velveteen coat
Black silk stock

Pavel

Scene 1
Ivory silk shirt
Stock #1
Wine coat
Same wig, moustache, boots, breeches

Scene 2
Same shirt, coat, boots
Change to wine stock
Beige w/rose print vest
Breeches

Scene 4
Same shirt, boots
Change to
Double brst black coat
Breeches
Grey/black stripe stock

Vassily

Scene 3
Same as I-3
Wool coat
Change to slippers

Prokofyich

Scene 2
Same as I-1
Wo/hat
Scene 4
Same as 2-2
Wo/coat

Piotr

Scene 1
Multi striped shirt
Tan silk breeches
Blue/black sash
Black shoes
Turquoise earring
Wig (LWT)

Scene 2
Same as I-1
Add rose livery vest (Burbank)

Timofeich

Scene 4
Ivory silk shirt (Murin)
Brown tweed breeches
Rust, wine pattern sash

Fedka

Scene 4
Brown print wool shirt
Tan silk breeches (Vale)
Adds boots

Piotr

Scene 1
Same as I-2
wo/vest

Scene 2
Same as 2-1

Scene 4
Same as 2-1

Timofeich

Scene 3
Same as I-3

Arina

Scene 3
Corset
Wig (LWT)
Petticoat
Avocado print dress
Black ankle boots
Amethyst necklace (personal)

Fenichka

Scene 1
Corset
Wig (personal)
Petticoat
Faded red & blue paisley dress
Print headscarf
Black ankle boots
Tights

Scene 2
Same corset, petticoat, wig, tights, boots
Tan w/red print dress

Anna

Scene 2
Corset
Wig (LWT)
Petticoat
Black evening gown
Black fabric pumps
Tights — black
Black gloves
Earrings
Black fan

Katya

Scene 2
Corset
Wig (Huntley)
Petticoat #1
Camisole
Ivory print dress
Ivory fabric pumps
White tights
Earrings

Princess

Scene 2
Corset
Wig (Huntley)
Petticoat
Black dress w/purple dots

Black pumps
Black knee-hi's
Black lace shawl
Necklace
Earrings

Dunyasha

Scene 1
Corset
Petticoat
Blouse #1
Tan silk skirt
Black & brown boots
Black tights
Apron

Scene 2
Same corset, petticoat, tights, boots
Blouse #1
Red print vest
Red print skirt

Arina

Scene 3
No corset & petticoat
Ivory nightgown
Beige slippers
Paisley shawl

Fenichka

Scene 1
Same corset, wig, petticoat, boots, tights
Ivory & navy paisley dress

Scene 2
Same as 2-1

Scene 4
Same corset, wig, boots, tights
Add piece to petticoat
Red paisley dress

Anna

Scene 1
Same corset, wig, petticoat
Champagne plaid silk dress
Light fabric shoes
Pearl earrings
White tights
Straw hat on set

Scene 4
Same corset, wig, petticoat, tights & shoes
Grey silk dress
Earrings

Katya

Scene 1
Same corset, wig, camisole
Petticoat #2
Green blouse
Floral print skirt
Leather sash
Black ankle boots (carry on)
No tights

Scene 4
Same corset, wig, camisole

Petticoat
Blue w/red paisley dress
Black ankle boots
Tights

Princess

Scene 4
Same corset, wig, petticoat, knee-hi's, shoes
Brown striped dress
Earrings

Dunyasha

Scene 1
Same corset, boots, petticoat
Blouse #2
Red print skirt

Scene 2
Same as 2-1

Scene 4
Same as 2-1

SET 2
S.L. WAGON
STORED

CEILING OVER

ACT I
S.L.
WAGON

PERM.
PLATFORM

ACT 2
S.R. WAGON
STORED

ACT I
S.R.
WAGON

RAMP UP

ACT I PLAN

" FATHERS & SONS "

SET 2 PLAN

"FATHERS & SONS"

Other Publications for Your Interest

THE BALLAD OF SOAPY SMITH
(ADVANCED GROUPS—EPIC COMIC DRAMA)
By MICHAEL WELLER

24 men, 9 women (with doubling)—Various interiors and exteriors (may be unit set)

"Col." Jefferson Randolph Smith, known as "Soapy" to his friends and foes, is a celebrated, notorious con man whose reputation has, alas, not preceded him to the Alaska Gold Rush town of Skagway in 1897, when the play takes place. Soapy is a charming gentleman, and he starts up a protection racket which brings law and order to the town, giving it a church and an infirmary. Oddly enough Soapy, the criminal, becomes a force for moral good; until the town's hypocrisy and vicious self interest bring him down, a victim of the cardinal sin of believing in his own con. "Michael Weller deserves praise for a historical play with contemporary relevance, daring to accost a large canvas. The protagonist is a complex and absorbing creation. I left the theatre, for once, thinking rather than trying to forget."—N.Y. Mag. "A rousing epic"—AP. "A good time on a grand scale, with a mind and vision of rare intensity."—Gannett/Westchester Newsp.   (#3975)

(Royalty, $60-40.)

HURLYBURLY
(ADVANCED GROUPS—DRAMA)
By DAVID RABE

4 men, 3 women—Interior

This rivetting new drama by the author of *The Basic Training of Pavlo Hummel, Sticks and Bones* and *Streamers* took New York by storm in a production directed by Mike Nichols and starring William Hurt, Sigourney Weaver, Judith Ivey, Christopher Walken, Harvey Keitel and Jerry Stiller. Quite a cast, and quite a play! The drama is the story of four men nosedeep in the decadent, perverted, cocaine-laden culture that is Hollywood; pursuing their sex-crazed, dope-ridden vision of the American Dream. "*Hurlyburly* offers some of Mr. Rabe's most inventive and disturbing writing. At his impressive best, Mr. Rabe makes grim, ribald and surprisingly compassionate comedy out of the lies and rationalizations that allow his alienated men to keep functioning (if not feeling) in the fogs of lotusland. They work in an industry so corrupt that its only honest executives are those who openly admit that they lie."—N.Y. Times. "Rabe has written a strange, bitterly funny, self-indulgent, important play."—N.Y. Post. "An important work, masterly accomplished."—Time. "A powerful permanent contribution to American drama . . . rivetting, disturbing, fearsomely funny . . . has a savage sincerity and a crackling theatrical vitality. This deeply felt play deserves as wide an audience as possible."—Newsweek.   (#10163)

(Royalty, $60-$40.)

Other Publications for Your Interest

LAKEBOAT

(ADVANCED GROUPS—COMEDY)

By DAVID MAMET

8 men—Unit set

This fascinating series of vignettes, staged to great acclaim by the Milwaukee Repertory Theatre, is set aboard a Great Lakes steamer, bound from Gary to Duluth. It focuses in on the eight-member crew, the hardhats of the steel waterways, all but one of whom are "lifers." The other character is a young college man who has been hired to replace the night cook. He is the elegant thing to the central figure. ". . . the show has much of Mamet's poetry of the inarticulate, the ritual, tribal double-talk that makes sense underneath the ludicrous patters of our lives."—Chicago Tribune. ". . . a banquet of meaty acting parts."—Milwaukee Sentinel.   (#14017)

(Royalty, $50–$35.)

GLENGARRY GLEN ROSS

(ADVANCED GROUPS—COMIC DRAMA)

By DAVID MAMET

7 men—2 Interiors

Winner of the London theatre equivalent of our Tony Award, this scalding comedy went on to take Broadway by storm, winning the Pulitzer Prize for drama in 1984. Never has Mr. Mamet's ear for the rhythms of actual, contemporary speech been more keen than in this tale of cutthroat real estate salesmen competing against each other for the money of unwary customers. One suavely vicious salesman, Richard Roma, is in the lead for the monthly sales award: a new Cadillac. Another, Shelly "The Machine" Levene, a former top salesman, is now riding a streak of bad luck on a smile and a shoeshine, hoping to turn his luck around. All are dependent upon an office manager named Williamson to give them the vital "leads" to new customers. Williamson, meanwhile, is pitting them against each other to drive up sales. In the first act, composed of three scenes, we meet the salesmen, vying for position as they gulp their cocktails in the local Chinese restaurant. The second act becomes a sort of "who done it" as the scene shifts to the office, where a burglary has taken place. The vital leads have been filched the night before, possibly by one of the salesmen. In the end, Williamson screws Roma out of his car and nabs the bag man. "Crackling tension . . . ferocious comedy and drama. A top American playwright in bristling form."—N.Y. Times. "Wonderfully funny . . . a play to see, remember and cherish."—N.Y. Post. "Mamet is . . . a pure writer, and the synthesis he appears to be making, with echoes from voices as diverse as Beckett, Pinter and Hemingway, is unique and exciting."—Newsweek.   (#9058)

(Royalty, $60–$40.)

Other Publications for Your Interest

THE CURATE SHAKESPEARE AS YOU LIKE IT
(LITTLE THEATRE—COMEDY)
By DON NIGRO

4 men, 3 women—Bare stage

This extremely unusual and original piece is subtitled: "The record of one company's attempt to perform the play by William Shakespeare". When the very prolific Mr. Nigro was asked by a professional theatre company to adapt *As You Like It* so that it could be performed by a company of seven he, of course, came up with a completely original play about a rag-tag group of players comprised of only seven actors led by a dotty old curate who nonetheless must present Shakespeare's play; and the dramatic interest, as well as the comedy, is in their hilarious attempts to impersonate all of Shakespeare's multitude of characters. The play has had numerous productions nationwide, all of which have come about through word of mouth. We are very pleased to make this "underground comic classic" widely available to theatre groups who like their comedy wide open and theatrical.   (#5742)

(Royalty, $50–$25.)

SEASCAPE WITH SHARKS AND DANCER
(LITTLE THEATRE—DRAMA)
By DON NIGRO

1 man, 1 woman—Interior

This is a fine new play by an author of great talent and promise. We are very glad to be introducing Mr. Nigro's work to a wide audience with *Seascape With Sharks and Dancer*, which comes directly from a sold-out, critically acclaimed production at the world-famous Oregon Shakespeare Festival. The play is set in a beach bungalow. The young man who lives there has pulled a lost young woman from the ocean. Soon, she finds herself trapped in his life and torn between her need to come to rest somewhere and her certainty that all human relationships turn eventually into nightmares. The struggle between his tolerant and gently ironic approach to life and her strategy of suspicion and attack becomes a kind of war about love and creation which neither can afford to lose. In other words, this is quite an offbeat, wonderful love story We would like to point out that the play also contains a wealth of excellent **monologue** and **scene material.**   (#21060)

(Royalty, $50–$35.)

Other Publications for Your Interest

BENEFACTORS
(LITTLE THEATRE—COMIC DRAMA)
By MICHAEL FRAYN

2 men, 2 women—Interior

Do not expect another *Noises Off*; here the multi-talented Mr. Frayn has more on his mind than Just Plain Fun. *Benefactors*, a long-running Broadway and London hit, is about doing good and do-gooding (not the same) and about the way the world changes outside your control just when you are trying to change it yourself. The story concerns an architect who has the sixties notion that if you give people good environments they will be good people. But, given a South London development to design, he is forced by town planners to go for a high-rise characterless scheme. No sooner does he begin to believe in this scheme than the fashion for high rises goes bust. ". . . one of the subtlest plays Broadway has seen in years, by one of the most extraordinary writers of the English-speaking theater . . . more political than most political plays, more intimate than most intimate plays and wiser than almost any play around today."—Newsweek. ". . . a fine . . . very good play . . . A Christmas present for theatergoers."—WABC-TV. ". . . a high point of the theater season . . . rare wit and intelligence."—Wall Street Journal. ". . . fascinating and astonishing play . . ."—N.Y. Daily News. ". . . dazzling and devastating play . . ."—N.Y. Times. ". . . a tour de force . . . simultaneously compelling and alienating . . ."—Christian Science Monitor. (#3980)

(Royalty, $60–$40.)

PACK OF LIES
(LITTLE THEATRE—DRAMA)
By HUGH WHITEMORE

3 men, 5 women—Combination interior

Bob and Barbara Jackson are a nice middle-aged English couple. Their best friends are their neighbors, Helen and Peter Kroger, who are Canadian. All is blissful in the protected, contained little world of the Jacksons; until, that is, a detective from Scotland Yard asks if his organization may use the Jackson's house as an observation station to try and foil a Soviet spy ring operating in the area. Being Good Citizens the Jacksons oblige, though they become progressively more and more put out as Scotland Yard's demands on them increase. They are really put to the test when the detective reveals to them that the spies are, in fact, their best friends the Krogers. Scotland Yard asks the Jacksons to cooperate with them to trap the spies, which really puts the Jacksons on the horns of a dilemma. Do they have the right to "betray" their friends? "This is a play about the morality of lying, not the theatrics of espionage, and, in Mr. Whitemore's view, lying is a virulent disease that saps patriots and traitors alike of their humanity."—N.Y. Times. "A crackling melodrama."—Wall St. Journal. "Absolutely engrossing . . . an evening of dynamic theatre."—N.Y. Post. "A superior British drama."—Chr. Sci. Mon. (#18154)

(Royalty, $60–$40.)